AF442687

SPIRITUALITY FOR FREEDOM

A HANDBOOK

S.K. MISHRA

ISBN
Paperback 979-8-89588-969-5
Hardcase 979-8-89632-744-8

*With the blessings of my late parents
and my late father-in-law and my mother-in-law,
I dedicate this book to my loving wife Susumna Mishra (Putli),
to my son-in-law Surya Narayan Das (Chintu),
to my daughter Sulina Mishra (Gudia),
and to my granddaughter Surlina Das (POTLI).*

God bless all.

CONTENTS

Who Should Read This Book — vii

Preface — ix

1. What Is Freedom — 1

2. Paramatman (Brahman Or Super Soul) — 3

3. Soul (Atman) — 5

4. What Are Ashta Siddhis — 8

5. Nava Nidhis — 17

6. Jnana And Bhakti — 25

7. Soul (Atman) — 30

8. Brahma Vidya: Imparted To Nachiketa By Yama Raj (God Of Death) — 33

9. Knowledge Of The Self - 3rd Boon For Nachiketa By Yama Raj — 35

10. Vidya And Avidya — 39

11. Yama Raj Talks About The State Of 'Desirelessness' — 42

12. Soul (Atma) Explained — 45

13. Super Soul: Param Atman — 46

14. Characteristics Of Devotees Who Know The Lord's Greatness — 48

15. Jivatma And Paramatma (Jiva And Brahma) — 50

16. Why The Indriyas Follow The Path Of Worldly Activities — 53

17. What Is Triguna And What Is Avyakta? — 57

18. Why The Creation Of The Indriyas Is Made By God — 62

19. What Happens When Knowledge Awakens In Human Beings — 65

20. What Happens When A Body Dies — 73

21. Which Aspirant Gets Happiness Being In The World   77

22. How The Jivatma Sees The Divine Swaroop Of Param Atman   86

23. Mind Gets Annihilated!   124

WHO SHOULD READ THIS BOOK

Yogis who are in the world yearning for liberation. The yogis who have left the world but are still slaves to their own vices such as greed, attachment, etc. All the persons who have strong dispassion and want to get rid of the unending cycles of birth and death. All who want to achieve God realisation through the processes of Spiritual Sadhana. All who believe in God.

All can become a yogi. It is not necessary that you go to a forest and practice yoga. Basically, persons having a spiritual bent of mind can become perfect yogis being in the world with families, relatives, and friends. Professionals like engineers, doctors, politicians, scientists, artists, lawyers, designers, constructors, businessmen etc. can practice spirituality to achieve all-round success. Everyone has a body, a mind, an intellect, ego, memory, and various sense organs. All of us have souls. No one is different from the other if we think that all have the same Atman (soul). What we lack is interest in reading the scriptures because our minds are elsewhere every time. We are so busy with worldly affairs that, while practicing spirituality within the hubbub of our daily business, we do not find time to step away from this ignorance and pursue real knowledge. Our scriptures say that we need to practice spirituality while doing all the work that form a part of our duties. Only then can we achieve real success. Words like Sama (concentrating our minds and efforts to get the desired results), Samadhan (maintaining steadfastness in accomplishing one's work without the distraction of the mind), and the like are described in the scriptures. It is said that one should resort to performing Purushartha or Spiritual Sadhana for the achievement of success and peace.

So dear readers of this book, please read all the lines written here, think through and reflect on the various topics described here. Do meditation and then start practicing. Let all be free from the clutches of maya (illusion and ignorance). Let all of us be elevated and meet with our dear God in this life. Please remember, if you do spiritual Sadhana in this birth and could not be successful, then in the next human birth God will permit you to resort to the Sadhana processes from the level you left in your earlier birth. But if you do not make efforts towards Spiritual Sadhana in this birth, it is not sure what will be your next birth. In human birth only, everyone can do Spiritual Sadhana. So, pray to God and start Spiritual Sadhana from now on without leaving your family nor stopping the performance of your own duties.

I have referred to the relevant Vedantas here. As we know, there are 108 Vedantas. Pick and choose is done by me so that we hit the point without reading all these scriptures.

OM!!! God bless you all!!! Hari Om tat Sat!!!

Om Peace! Om peace! Om Peace!

PREFACE

This is a thought-provoking and inspirational text. All of us are working and have little scope to think about real freedom. We are basically working from our minds. Just think, the sequence as described here:

We hear, touch, see, smell and/or taste something, and by that time, our respective sensory nerves send the signals to their own orb/s. This orb or the nerve center resides in our brain. The sensory nervous system detects, relays, and processes sensory information from the outside world to our brains. These 5 sense organs are known as Pancha Jnanendriya (Sabda-hear, sparsa-touch, rupa-vision, rasa-taste, Gandha-smell). The information thus received from the orb by our brain (our mind, the memory, and the intellect) is deciphered and analysed, and subsequent actions are taken by us through the respective motor nerve. There are 5 motor nerves, and they are known as Pancha Karmendriyas (Vaak-speech, paani-hands, paadau-hands, upastha-the urine excretory organ, paayu-the solid waste excretory organ).

The soul is the master of our body. We will discuss our soul in detail later. It is necessary for the soul to direct the intellect, the intellect to direct the mind, and the mind to direct the respective Karmendriya to act. However, there is a disconnect. We act based on the directives given by our minds. This is where we make a mistake. As a result of this, the wishes of our souls are ignored.

As we continuously ignore the wishes of our souls, we do not exactly know what we want. Hence, we become ignorant, and because of this ignorance, we are in continuous suffering owing to sorrows and pains, etc.

If we understand that all our sufferings are due to our own ignorance, we will try to avoid performing undesirable activities and strive for an elevated life. This way, we will be able to have freedom even while living in our present body.

There are specific injunctions and proper paths shown by our scriptures (Vedantas). We need to know these and perform our activities to be free. We may come from any stream such as engineering, medicine, arts, architecture, science, politics, et al. Spiritual knowledge is necessary for all of us to be free.

Each person, irrespective of their position, is supposed to manage every activity with spirituality. We will discuss all these lifestyles as we go ahead. A farmer, an industrialist, a homemaker, a retired person, a grocer, etc., all need to adopt the path of spirituality so that they can be free in this life. This is the beauty of the path of spirituality. We should remember that every action of ours will yield results. If the actions are proper and oriented towards goodness with no balance of actions, then only reactions owing to such actions will no longer be there. Up to this point, we already know that due to our ignorance, we commit sins. These sins result in pain and suffering. To have no suffering during this life, we need to have knowledge of the Vedantas. The Vedantic texts impart knowledge to us. By practicing the various injunctions, freedom from all worries will be achievable.

WHAT IS FREEDOM

Let us think with calm minds - "What do we want in reality?" Well, it is not very difficult to find out. Just let me give you some examples.

In a primary school, what happens when 'the last bell of the day' rings? The students come out of their classes and run frantically. This scene is very interesting to watch. A minute before the last bell rings, the students were studying. This means all the children want to be free from the studies. Just think!

If a person opens the door of a cage, all the birds inside the cage rush out and fly with great happiness. Lo! One can well understand that no living beings like to be bound.

Let us analyse these 2 events. All of us can say unanimously, 'We need freedom.'

When we are bound, we are not independent. So, we are sad. But on the contrary, we are happy when we are free. This is mainly because whenever we act on our own without anyone's interference, we are independent.

Let us say I am independent, but am I free? The answer is 'NO'.

Let me explain this: We need air to breathe, water to drink, food to eat, and land to walk, sleep, and stay. All these needs are very necessary for us to survive. Let us say these basic things are not available to us. No one is binding you. There is no interference in your activities. Are you free? Think! After some deep thought, you get the answer by yourself in the negative. Basically, from the moment our own self lies in the womb of our mother until our death, we are bound! But we need freedom. Do we have a way to be free while in life, or for that matter, while we are born until we die?

Here I remember the sentence of Jean-Jacques Rousseau, the famous Genevan philosopher, writer, and composer: "Man is born free, but everywhere he is in chains." What this philosopher means by 'Man' is the human being. He says though human beings are born without any tethers on them, they are still bound.

Let us go a little beyond. We live in a society. We must abide by the rules of our society. Even God must be disciplined if He has an incarnation on Earth. All the great men/women, irrespective of householders, all the emperors, all warriors, all workers, all saints, and all living beings that come to mind are to manage themselves as per the underlying environmental rules and regulations.

So, how to become free!

What do the scriptures say and promulgate?

The scriptures, basically the Vedantas, guide us methodically on how to overcome worldly sorrows.

As a matter of fact, IGNORANCE is the root cause of all sorrows. Almost all seers have become free by studying the Vedantas and by strictly abiding by the injunctions laid down there.

There is a beautiful stanza written by Adi Shankar:

Vedaantaarth Vichaarena Jaayate Jnaanamuttamam,

Tenaatyantik sansara duhkhanaso bhabatyanu.

Supreme wisdom arises from understanding the meaning of the Vedanta texts. Following these texts, one can annihilate worldly sorrows entirely.

There are 108 known Vedantas. If we want freedom in this life and in the henceforth lives, till final emancipation, we need to read and follow the Vedantas. We can gain real knowledge from the Vedantas.

Let us discuss various topics one by one to understand what path is ordained in the Vedantas to achieve freedom.

PARAMATMAN (BRAHMAN OR SUPER SOUL)

The scriptures describe Paramatman or Super Soul (Brahman) and Atman or soul. If you think that the whole universe is a capsule, then this capsule is pervaded by Paramatman. All creations, maintenance, and destructions are performed by the powers of Paramatman. He is very powerful. So, we know Him as Omnipotent. He is immobile and knowledgeable. He is all-pervasive, and that is why He is Omnipresent. He has all knowledge, and as a matter of fact, all knowledge ensues from Him, and hence, we call Him omniscient.

Because of His powers, the whole universe exists. His characteristics are described as:

He moves (for the unwise), and He is immobile (for the erudite); He does what He feels or thinks to do. Only entities having absolute freedom can do this.

He is here and He is also present at a distance. He is present inside and also present outside. So, we say that He is Omnipresent.

He is not affected by diseases. He is free from all sorrows. He is pure and perfect. He has a speed that is better than all that we know. He has the speed better than the mind. He can reach anywhere before our mind reaches there. He is very kind and impartial.

He illumines by Himself. He provides light to all. All beings have knowledge from Him only. He remains forever. He is always satisfied. We do not have to offer any food to appease His appetite because He has no appetite. Brahman is not limited to an idol. Persons with knowledge and extreme dispassion can get Him provided they do PURUSHARTHA (A spiritual practice for Soul Elevation). A person who is well-established in Brahman is not bound.

Brahman is the source of this universe. As a rosary has beads, similarly, many worlds are hung from Brahman. As a human being has numerous, uncountable vellus hair, similarly, Brahman holds numerous, uncountable worlds. This Brahman is also known as Param Purush. Brahman is the one and only one. He resides in all living and non-living entities. He has created all laws concerning the creation, maintenance, and annihilation of various worlds. He strictly abides by His framed rules without deviation. He is beyond all characteristics (Sarva-gunadhaari). Brahman keeps everything under His control. Anyone who sees Him inside his body gets peace. All others are devoid of peace. This Brahman, who has so many characteristics, is unknowable. Since Brahman is invisible in ourselves, getting a glimpse is possible by the following method:

Think of OM as a bow. Now, our soul is the arrow. Now shoot the arrow to the target, which is Brahman. This way, it is possible (as stated by the Vedantas) to get a glimpse of Brahman.

SOUL (ATMAN)

All of us identify ourselves as our body. But this body is temporary. Inside our body, we have the master of our body, and this is known as the soul. As we go ahead, we will try to understand more about our soul. This is also known as our Spirit. As we know more about our soul and try our best to understand its own characteristics, we will be able to comprehend what our Spirit or our soul wants. If we make continuous efforts to elevate our souls, we will be able to completely free ourselves from the tethers of the cycle of myriad births and deaths. This SPIRITUAL PROCESS is known as Soul Elevation. Many spiritual aspirants work incessantly towards the elevation of their own souls.

For now, we have some understanding about the Super Soul. As the Super Soul or the Brahman is omnipresent, so our soul is part and parcel of the Super Soul. When the Super Soul is a set of souls, the reverse is not true. It means that the Super Soul or the Brahman is the source of all souls. The souls reside in various bodies. All living beings have a soul inside their bodies. The soul departs as soon as the body dies. In all living beings, at the time of departure, the souls carry the mind, intellect, ego, and memory (Antahkarans or tanmaatras) along with themselves. In living beings lower than human beings, such as animals, the power of discrimination is either absent or has very little presence, which can be ignored.

Because of a very wrong decision, the souls depart from the Super Souls and get into the wombs of living beings. Human wombs are the superior most among all wombs. So, getting into the womb of a human being by any soul takes many uncountable years. The soul is bound by the body and is kicked up and down continuously by the breath. Hence, the souls have no happiness inside the living beings. Knowing this, the spiritual aspirants always strive for the conscious departure of their souls from their bodies. These souls that get away from any human body consciously are known as elevated souls. These elevated souls ride and rest on higher and higher levels till they mingle with the Super Soul and are permanently free.

As a matter of fact, there are 7 higher levels: Bhuh, Bhuvah, Swah, Maha, Janah, Tapah and finally Satyam. The soul of a human body resides in the Bhuh level or the Bhuh layer. Bhuh is our Earth. Human beings are superior to all the other living beings and are suitable to know themselves. Knowing thyself, these human beings can elevate their own souls. If a human being dies without realising his/her own self, then after death, such an ignorant being gets into a lower womb to take birth. Many a time, the souls, due to their ignorance, after departing a body, enter darkness or a black hole.

This reminds me of a story of Lord Krishna during His childhood after He completed His education from His Guru, namely Sandipani. Please listen carefully.

Guru Sandipani had his wife named Gautami. They had a son who died long ago. After Lord Krishna and His elder brother Lord Balarama completed their spiritual studies from Guru Ji, as a gesture of gratitude, they asked their guru to express his wishes before them so that they could fulfil his wishes as Guru Dakshina. Upon hearing this, Guru Sandipani did not ask for anything because he knew that Lord Krishna and Lord Balarama were the incarnations of God. Basically, we are not to ask anything of God because God knows everything, and He is very merciful. He bestows upon us what we deserve.

However, his wife Gautami told Lord Krishna to bring back their son, who had expired long ago. Lord Krishna felt very happy and went in search of their son. He found his son lying in a black hole. He went there and lifted their son from the dungeon. Thus, the son of His Guru could come back to life. Such an action can only be performed by God. Giving life to the dead is a Siddhi. This Siddhi is known as Ishitwam. We also know that Lord Hanuman had Ashta Siddhi. There are 18 known siddhas who also mastered Aṣhta Siddhis.

In the Vedantas, it is very clearly written, "A human being who dies without realising the self goes to the level of darkness after death. This level is known as Asurya, meaning thereby where there is neither intellect nor brilliancy." This statement verily instructs and encourages everyone to go through the process of Soul Elevation or perform Purushartha to know thyself.

As we strictly perform Purushartha, we become yogis. On this path, we acquire many siddhis. But these siddhis are not to be told nor shown to anyone. A yogi who either tells or shows his spiritual powers to others, his achievement to acquire higher levels stops there.

We say that Lord Hanuman bestows Ashta Siddhi and Nava Nidhi (Eight siddhis and Nine Nidhis). Let us understand what these siddhis are.

Siddhis are godly powers. Great yogis and obviously Gods and their incarnations possess Ashta Siddhis and Nava Nidhis. When a yogi elevates his own soul by the performance of Purushartha (Soul Elevation Process), he/she gets the various siddhis and the Nidhis one by one. You must have known that a great saint, namely Swami Samarth, was able to give life to the dead. Similarly, Saint Tulsidas also had Ishitwam Siddhi.

WHAT ARE ASHTA SIDDHIS

As the name suggests, Ashta means 8. The 8 siddhis are:

1. ANIMA SIDDHI:

Of all the eight siddhis, ANIMMA is the first Siddhi. An accomplished yogi or a deity having this Siddhi can shrink his or her body to the minimum possible. The body can be shrunk to a cell even by this Siddhi. But to come back to the original shape, one must have the other Siddhi, which is known as MAHIMA Siddhi. As a matter of fact, a yogi who has acquired ANIMA Siddhi, by the way, must have acquired the MAHIMA Siddhi. Lord Hanuman used ANIMA Siddhi many times. He used this Siddhi to find out Sita Mata in Lanka. When Lord Rama and Lakshman were kidnapped by Mahiravan and taken to sacrifice before his deity, Lord Hanuman went to Patal, and during this time, He used this Siddhi again to search for Lord Rama and Lakshman.

2. MAHIMA SIDDHI:

This Siddhi complements ANIMA. In this Siddhi, the accomplished yogi can expand his/her body to any size, however large it could be. So, anyone who has the ANIMA SIDDHI must have the MAHIMA Siddhi.

We have known Dasavatara (Matsya, Kurma, Varaha, Narasimha, Vamana, Parasurama, Rama, Balaram, Buddha, and Kalki) of Lord Vishnu. Vamana showed this MAHIMA Siddhi to push Mahavali to Patala. During this time, Lord Vishnu took birth in a Brahmin's house. He took the incarnation as a dwarf. On one occasion, He went to the palace of King Mahavali to receive donations. At that time, King Mahavali was very famous throughout the world as a very merciful and great donor. But anything in excess is not proper as per the laws of nature. So, Lord Vishnu, in the incarnation of Vamana, by showing His MAHIMA Siddhi, could completely occupy heaven on one foot and use the other foot, and He completely occupied the Earth. King Mahavali was very surprised. Due to his powers of magnanimity, he could conquer both the heaven and the Earth. As soon as Vamana occupied both worlds, Mahavali asked God to show him the third foot. Immediately thereafter, the Lord created the third foot arising from His navel. Then King Mahavali showed his head. Lord Vamana pressed King Mahavali to Patala by putting His third foot on his head.

There is another example of MAHIMA Siddhi shown by Lord Hanuman. When Hanuman was asked by Lord Rama to collect Vishalya Karani, the medicinal herb Gandhamadana, a mountain peak in the Himalayas, he could not recognise the herb. He became very large by His MAHIMA Siddhi to lift Gandhamadana.

3. LAGHIMA SIDDHI:

A siddha having this Siddhi can make his body as light as possible. With this Siddhi, one can perform levitation and easily fly in the sky. Great siddhas have this power. Levitation was shown by Lord Hanuman many times. He flew from place to place to accomplish various tasks. He had to fly over the ocean to reach Lanka. This is the power of LAGHIMA Siddhi.

4. GARIMA SIDDHI:

This is complementary to LAGHIMA Siddhi. The siddha can increase the weight to any extent.

This Siddhi was shown by the monkey Prince Angad. Before the war between Lord Rama and the demon Ravan, Prince Angad was sent by Lord Rama as a messenger to have peace and avoid the imminent war. During that time, in the court of the demon King Ravan, Angad and Lord Rama were humiliated. Not tolerating the humiliating words against Lord Rama, Angad used Garima Siddhi and asked all the demons, including Ravan, to lift one of his feet. Due to the blessings of Lord Rama, no one could lift the foot of Angad.

Lord Hanuman also showed Garima Siddhi to eliminate the ego of Bheem, the second brother of the Pandavas. Hanuman had to use this Siddhi as Lord Krishna required. During the Mahabharat war, Bheem was asked by Lord Krishna to invite Lord Hanuman to help them in the Mahabharat war. Lord Hanuman belonged to the age of Treta (Satya/Kreta Yuga is known as the Golden Age, Treta Yuga is known as the Silver Age, Dwapar is known as the Bronze Age, and Kali is known as the Iron age. All of us belong to the Iron age). He has all siddhis. When Bheem came to meet him, he was sitting on the road with his tail lying fully across it. Bheem saw the old monkey. He told him to give him a way by taking out his tail from the road. But Hanuman made his tail very heavy by applying Garima Siddhi and told Bheem to lift his tail and go. Hanuman said, "I have become very old. It is very difficult on my part to lift my tail." Bheem took his words lightly and tried to lift the tail of Hanuman. He could not do so. Finally, he understood all about his ego and felt the same. He begged excuse before Lord Hanuman. This way, Lord Krishna could eliminate Bheem's ego.

SIMULTANEOUS DISPLAY OF MAHIMA AND LAGHIMA SIDDHI SHOWN BY LORD KRISHNA:

Lord Krishna was the king of Dwarka. He is known as Krishna Dwaipayana. He had 8 consorts. Apart from Rukmini, who was the incarnation of Mahalakshmi, another queen was Satyabhama. Satyabhama was a very beautiful woman. Her father was also very rich. Once upon a time, Satyabhama helped Lord Krishna during His war with Narakasura. Because of all these reasons, she had a lot of ego. Lord Krishna could sense this, and He requested Narada to help Him reduce Satyabhama's ego to the bare minimum.

Accordingly, Narada came to meet Lord Krishna in Dwarka. During that time, Satyabhama came to greet Narada and comfort him as she usually did for all the guests. Narada was very happy. Satyabhama asked Narada, "Dear Devarshi (Narada was known as Devarshi because he was both a demigod and a rishi), can you please bless me so that I can have Lord Krishna as my husband in all my births on Earth!" Listening to this, Narada asked her, "Is it possible for you to give Lord Krishna to serve me in this birth?" Without thinking about the pros and cons of the matter, she immediately agreed to give Lord Krishna to Narad Ji. After some time, she understood the repercussions. During that time, all the other 7 queens came there. Narada was taking Lord Krishna to his abode. Seeing this, Satyabhama was very worried. She immediately asked Narada to give Lord Krishna back. But Narada did not agree. He said, "If you want me to return Lord Krishna, then you need to give me gold equal to the weight of Lord Krishna." Satyabhama was very relieved to hear such a solution from Narada Ji.

Then, a balance was organised. Lord Krishna sat on one pan. On the other pan, gold bars and gold ornaments were kept in equal measure. But lo! The pan where Lord Krishna was sitting remained unmoved on the ground. Satyabhama was quite surprised at this scene. She was very perturbed. Not finding any solution, she asked the eldest of all the queens, Rukmini, to help her. Rukmini said, "You can place a basil leaf over the gold and get the matter solved." Immediately thereafter, Satyabhama collected a basil leaf from the yard and placed it on the heap of gold kept on the other pan. To everyone's surprise, the pan where Lord Krishna was sitting was suddenly raised, and balance was achieved. Through this, Satyabhama could let go of her ego, and from that day onwards, she had no ego regarding wealth and beauty.

In this story, Lord Krishna displayed both MAHIMA and LAGHIMA siddhis. When the pan was down, he displayed MAHIMA SIDDHI, and when the balance was raised with the basil leaf on the other pan, he displayed LAGHIMA SIDDHI.

5. PRAPTI SIDDHI:

This Siddhi is acquired, which is not concerning with the body as discussed earlier. In this Siddhi, the Gods, Demigods, great saints and even demons were getting materials whatsoever they desire from the thin air.

Let me give you one example here of how great saints could get materials from thin air. There was a great saint named Trailingeshwara. He was a great saint and could acquire lots of spiritual powers. He was living in Benares. On one occasion, he was going with the king of Banaras in a boat in the river water of the Ganges. The king was carrying a golden sword with him. He had a great amount of ego due to the sword. Swami Trailingeshwara could sense this. He asked the king to show him his golden sword. The king obliged and gave the saint his sword to examine it. Intentionally, the saint dropped the sword into the deep waters of the river Ganges. They were sailing amidst the riverbed. The king became very angry with the saint. He said it was not proper on the part of the saint to drop the sword in the river water. Swami Ji heard everything and put his hand into the water from the boat and retrieved 4 such golden swords from the river water. Then, showing the swords to the king, he asked the king, "Please recognise your sword from these 4 swords." Upon this, the king was very surprised and felt deeply ashamed. He immediately begged for forgiveness from the saint for his own folly and ego.

Here, Swami Trailingeshwara displayed PRAKAMYA SIDDHI.

Gods and demigods, when pleased with anyone, give divine gifts brought from thin air. During wartime, the demigods and demons get weapons from thin air.

6. PRAKAMYA SIDDHI:

This is a very great Siddhi. With this Siddhi, Rishis and demigods are adept in any atmosphere. They can live long, float on water, and stay underwater for extended periods. This increases their longevity.

There is a story about Lord Mahadeva in this Siddhi. We all know that Saturn Mahadasa lasts for 19 years. Everyone must pass through all the Mahadasas of the 9 planets: Sun-6 years, Moon-10 years, Mars-7 years, Mercury-17 years, Jupiter-16 years, Venus 20 years, Saturn 19 years, Rahu 18 years, and Ketu 7 years. Thus, the total number of years becomes 120 years. When anyone lives beyond 120 years, the various Mahadasas get repeated one by one. The sequence of the Mahadasas is Sun, Moon, Mars, Rahu, Jupiter, Saturn, Mercury, Ketu, and Venus. So, in the case of Mahadeva, Saturn Mahadasa was about to come. Saturn came to visit the Lord to alert Him. All know that Saturn Mahadasa gives bad results. A little undisciplined act could prove very bad; Saturn does not tolerate indiscipline. As a precautionary measure, Lord Mahadeva stayed inside sea water for 19 years. On completion of 19 years, Lord Mahadeva came out of the seawater. Just at that time, Saturn was waiting for the Lord to come out. He said to Saturn, "You could not do any harm to me because I was inside the sea." After listening to the statements of Mahadeva, Saturn smiled and said, "My dear Lord, during my reign of 19 years in your life, I made you stay inside seawater. What more trouble could it be beyond this!"

Hence, from this example, you can understand how Lord Mahadeva was displaying PRAKAMYA Siddhi.

Swami Trailingeshwara was able to stay inside the water of the river Ganges for 6 months at a stretch.

7. VASHITWAM SIDDHI:

This is, again, a very amazingly great Siddhi. In this Siddhi, the yogis and demigods possess such powers. The holder of this power can control the minds of others, human beings, animals, birds, trees, and even the non-living. The siddha is able to tame wild animals, beasts, and any living creature that is insane or wayward.

The youngest of all the Pandavas was Sahadeva. He had the VASHITWAM Siddhi. After the completion of 12 years of banishment, the Pancha Pandavas had to stay incognito for one year. They chose the place of King Virat of Virat Nagar (Now Nepal) to spend this year in an incognito state.

One by one, the Pandavas met King Virat and introduced themselves, explaining their skills and how they served King Yudhishthira of Indraprastha. King Virat was very pleased to accept them and deployed them in his kingdom as per the skill set of the Pandavas, starting with Yudhishrthira. When Sahadeva's turn came, he mentioned his ability to influence the minds of living and non-living beings, making them act as he wished. He expressed his desire to be a cowherd and care for all the king's cows. King Virat informed Sahadeva that King Indra had taken all his one-lakh cows to heaven and asked if he could bring them back. Sahadeva agreed and played his flute. The melodious sound summoned the cows from heaven. Impressed, King Virat kept

Sahadeva in his palace to look after his cows. This demonstrates the power of VASHITWAM SIDDHI.

Lord Krishna was the master of all these siddhis. He was performing many miracles during His childhood days in Gopa. There were 1 lakh and 60 thousand Gopis. He was able to attract the Gopis by playing His flute. The sound of His flute was so enchanting that the Gopis flocked to the place where the Lord was playing the flute. They stopped all their domestic chores during that time. It was only due to the power of VASHITWAM SIDDHI.

8. ISHITWAM SIDDHI:

This is a great power. The owner of this power can change the climate, can move large objects like the Earth, can bring in rain, can get water filled in a dry well. In a similar manner, the siddha can be able to stop rain and natural hazards. By this Siddhi, one can give life to the dead. This Siddhi is only there with great saints like Mahavatar Babaji, Swami Samarth, Tulsi Das, Santh Gnaneshwar, Lahiri Mahasaya, Gorakhnath, Matshyendranath, etc.

If you have read the book 'An Autobiography of a Yogi' written by Yogananda Paramhansa, you must have known this story just written by me here:

On one occasion, a great devotee of Mahavatar Babaji went to the Himalayas to meet him. He knew that Babaji stayed in the Himalayas in a cave of Dronagiri. He went there. It was an evening when he reached Dronagiri. Babaji came there and asked the devotee, "Why have you come here risking your life?" The devotee said, "I want to meet Babaji." Babaji replied, "It is not easy to meet him. Please go back." The devotee then replied, "I would prefer to die by jumping from here than to go back." Babaji said, "Then you better jump because Babaji does not like to meet you." The man was very depressed listening to the words of the man. He immediately jumped from there and died. Babaji was greatly moved by the devotion of this devotee. He immediately sent 2 of his disciples to find out the man and bring him to his cave. The disciples found the dead body and brought it to Babaji's cave. Babaji touched the dead body and made him alive. All his wounds and pain were no longer there. He was feeling extremely comfortable. This way Babaji exhibited ISHITWAM SIDDHI. As a matter of fact, He is a great siddha and is now more than 1800 years of age. He is called 'The ageless monk'. He taught Kriya Yoga to his disciple Lahiri Mahasaya and allowed him to pass on the knowledge of Kriya Yoga to worldly aspirants. His mantra is "OM KRIYA BABAJI NAMAH OM."

Lord Krishna showed many miracles during His childhood. One example of His ISHITWAM Siddhi is rescuing a hunchbacked woman. She was a true devotee of Lord Krishna, who lived in Mathura. When Lord Krishna and His elder brother Lord Balarama were going to attend Dhanu Utsav organised by the cruel King Kansa in Mathura, on their way, they came across a woman with a hunchback. She was so overjoyed to see the 2 brothers that she wanted to give them sandal paste, and she put it on their heads with great sincerity. Lord Krishna was moved by her devotion and touched her back. The woman was rescued, her hunchback was straightened, and she regained her real beautiful appearance. This is due to ISHITWAM SIDDHI.

Let us know another great story of how Lord Shiva could give life to Daksh Prajapati:

There is a nice story of Lord Shiva and Daksh Prajapati. Daksh was one of the manas putras (sons/daughters being created by mere thought waves). He was the king of the Himalayas. He had 2 daughters. The youngest was named Sati. She was extremely beautiful. Daksh wanted to get her married to Lord Vishnu. But Sati had the sole interest of marrying Lord Shiva. She was very much attracted by the great powers, wisdom, and mercifulness of Lord Shiva. The only shortcomings of Lord Shiva are that He stays in the graveyard, wears the ashes of the burnt bodies and has a snake around His neck. He wears a very small amount of clothes just to cover His lower part. His body, though very handsome, He does not care about. He is usually engrossed in meditation and maintains strict Brahmacharya. All these characteristics attracted Sati Mata. Daksh hated Lord Shiva owing to His attire only. Sati took on extreme austerities in the Himalayan Forest to propitiate

Lord Shiva. Owing to her deep love, Lord Shiva agreed to marry Sati. The marriage took place, and Lord Shiva took Sati to his place of stay in the Himalayas.

Daksh wanted to perform a Yagna (Yagna is a holy activity to propitiate God and to purify oneself from sins). He invited all the demigods, Lord Vishnu and Lord Brahma, to attend the Yagna. But he did not invite Sati and Lord Shiva. Knowing this, Sati wanted to attend the function without an invitation. Lord Shiva refused to let Sati attend the function. But Sati did not listen to the advice of Lord Shiva. Seeing Sati in the place where the Yagna was performed, Daksh got very angry and talked impolitely to Sati and expressed very bad words against Lord Shiva. Sati could not tolerate the humiliation of her husband, and owing to this, she immediately jumped into the holy fire of the Yagna and was burnt.

Lord Shiva could know about this event. He loved Sati very much. He came to the place where Sati was burnt. He was very furious and created a character from His hair that was equivalent to Himself, namely Veerabhadra. He also invoked Bhadrakali from the clutch of His hair. Veerabhadra beheaded Daksh with his sword. Bhadrakali, along with her Bhutaganas, ransacked the place and killed everyone who fought against them. The Yagna was destroyed fully.

Thereafter, the wife (Prashuti, mother of Sati) of Daksh, who was also the mother of Sati, beseeched Lord Shiva to bring back Daksh to life. Lord Shiva was pacified. He got a goat's head and fitted it on the neck of Daksh Prajapati and gave him life. This way, He smashed the ego of Daksh Prajapati. This is due to ISHITWAM.

Friends and dear spiritual aspirants, God is always kind. He is all-merciful and impartial. He does not like anyone having ego, cruelty, violence, and other bad qualities. He always takes the pain to come to Earth and to the other worlds to save His devotees from the clutches of the demons. Pray to the Lord with heart and soul and make all-out efforts for Soul Elevation.

NAVA NIDHIS

As the name suggests, Nava Nidhis are 9 spiritual perfections. They are less powerful than the Ashta Siddhis, but to have these Nidhis, yogis undergo serious processes to achieve these powers. Gods, incarnations of Gods, some demigods, and great acclaimed saints acquire Nava Nidhis.

Usually, Nidhis refer to treasure or wealth. According to the epics, Kuber is the demigod in charge of the treasure of heaven.

Let us list out the Nava Nidhis first. They are:

Padma Nidhi, Mahapadma Nidhi, Nila Nidhi, Sankha Nidhi, Makar Nidhi, Kachchhapa Nidhi, Mukunda Nidhi, Nanda Nidhi, and Kharva Nidhi.

These are spiritual assets. To acquire these Nidhis, an aspirant must perform deep spiritual practices with devotion and sincerity. Only then will the blessings of the Almighty shower on the spiritual aspirant.

In Ramayan, we know that Sita Mata bestowed Ashta Siddhi and Nava Nidhi to Lord Hanuman due to his deep devotion to Lord Rama.

The Nava Nidhis are the 9 prime energies or forces of the universe. Nava Grahas (Sun, Moon, Mars, Mercury, Jupiter, Venus, Saturn, Rahu, and Ketu) guard these treasures for the possessor of the Nava Nidhis. Wealth, prosperity, and good fortune ensue with Nava Nidhis. Let us discuss these Nidhis one by one:

1. Padma Nidhi:

   Padma is a lotus flower. During reincarnations, this Nidhi stays with the possessor. A person with pure Sattva qualities can earn this Nidhi. Qualities of ethics, truth, honesty, and righteousness are the basis to achieve this Nidhi. Gold and silver are acquired by having this Nidhi. These treasures can be passed on to generations. All sattvic persons of the family can possess this wealth. They must donate for good work as mandatory to have this Nidhi.

2. Mahapadma Nidhi:

Maha means great or large. The wealth acquired by the Sattviki stays for 7 generations. Simply possessing these Nidi does not qualify the person. He/she needs to share and donate the treasure to others who are deserving.

3. Nila Nidhi:

These Nidhis cover sapphire and gemstones. People with both Sattvik and Rajasic Gunas can have these treasures. Their riches remain for 3 generations. People must do trading also to acquire these properties. Many a time some cunning persons also do perfect trading and accumulate these treasures. The possessions of these people are held in due respect by others.

4. Shankh Nidhi;

Sankha means a conch shell. Usually, very selfish people earn this, Nidhi. They earn for themselves and do not even spend the riches for the betterment of their family. Wealth is their God only.

5. Makara Nidhi:

As the name suggests, Makara means the crocodile. A person with tamasic qualities possesses these treasures. Usually, they acquire swords and other armaments to engage in a fight or quarrel with others. They often pick fights with their employers. Such people also die with weapons.

6. Kachchhapa Nidhi:

Kachchhapa means tortoise. These individuals acquire great wealth. However, they are very miserly in nature. They do not spend money even on themselves. Like a Kachchhapa conceals its head in the shell, similarly, they keep their treasure in a secret place.

7. Mukunda Nidhi:

Mukunda is a naturally occurring metal known as cinnabar or mercury, which is a heavy metal that remains liquid at room temperature. Pure Rajasic persons have this treasure with them. They have acquired this treasure suddenly from somewhere. This treasure remains with them for one generation only. They do not possess any sattvic qualities like truthfulness, honesty, or mercifulness. They have this treasure only during their lifetime.

8. Nanda Nidhi:

Nanda means pleasure. These people who possess these Nidhis have both sattvic and rajasic qualities. They have a long life and they are also involved in sharing and donating their wealth owing to the sattvic qualities. They are ambitious and they progress in their life in a steady manner. They need appreciation and self-respect also.

9. Kharva Nidhi:

Kharva indicates cups or countless aspects. These persons have all the other 8 treasures but in small quantities. They are very clever and know the techniques of acquiring the wealth of others. By acquiring others' wealth, these people like to live a luxurious life.

MINOR SIDDHIS:

Siddhis usually have the objective of making the self-free from the worldly bondages. Ashta Siddhis are the major siddhis as we discussed. Other than these siddhis, there are quite a few minor siddhis. These siddhis are clearly described in the Vedantas (Yoga Kaundilya Upanishad).

God and His incarnations have these siddhis because God is the source of all siddhis, and their incarnations inherit various major and minor siddhis from God. Most demigods and acclaimed saints possess minor siddhis. This is because, to attain the level of demigods, they had undergone stricter disciplines and Soul Elevation processes earlier.

When a yogi practices yoga with the help of a guru, during the performance of such processes, they acquire many minor siddhis unknowingly. A spiritual power, namely KUNDALINI, awakens during various yogic practices. It is stated in the Vedantas that a serpent is coiled by 2 and a half coils and is in a dormant state placed in the groove of the Mooladhara. Mooladhara is a plexus in our body which is placed just at the end of our backbone. The other 5 plexuses are known as Swadhisthan, about 2 inches above the Mooladhara. At the navel, there is also a plexus known as Manipura, and the plexus in the heart is known as Anahata. Similarly, the plexus at the throat centre is known as Visuddhi. On the tip of the nose, another plexus is present. This is a very important plexus known as Ajna. It controls our internalities, which we call Antahkarans. The main 4 internalities are known as mind, intellect, ego, and memory (Manas, Buddhi, Ahamkara, and Chitta). All of us perform real activities according to the instructions of the Antahkarans. All nerves going to the brain from all parts of our body are conglomerated in the plexus. A person who has a well-developed Ajna plexus can perform spiritual practices for Soul Elevation. To work towards this requires great determination and resolution, apart from the blessings of God.

The seventh plexus is known as the Sahasrar Plexus. It is placed on the top of our head, and the centre of this plexus is known as Brahma-Randra. Please remember, during our birth, right near our head, near our forehead, was a small place which was very soft and was not filled by our skull bone. As time passes, this soft point moves towards the top of our heads and finally becomes hard. This now remains a very small invisible hole. We call this hole the Brahma-Randra.

The air that we breathe in and out is of 5 types – (1. Prana; 2. Apana; 3. Vyana; 4. Udana; and 5. Samana). The Udana Vayu flows from the lower portion of our body to the higher planes of consciousness. For example, when we yawn, the Udana Vayu flows. The yogis perform great sadhanas to orient the flow of Udana Vayu from Mooladhara to the Sahasrar through the Sushumna Nadi. If the yogi becomes successful in tending the Udana Vayu flow from Mooladhara in the passage of Sushumna Nadi, then he/she can become free from the repeated births and deaths in this world. But it is still not known at which level the soul rests. The basic aim is to elevate the soul to the Satya Loka.

Representation of the 7 chakras or the 7 plexuses in the flute of Lord Krishna:

All the scriptures can be analysed from the Pinda-Brahmanda concept. All the images of various Gods and Goddesses and their equipment/armaments, their shapes, colours, dresses, etc., are to be analysed deeply so that what is present there in our body is represented through stories or through symbols to represent the Sharira Tattva (philosophy of Pinda or the body).

You must have seen Lord Krishna holding a flute. The flute has 6 holes and a larger hole towards the end from where the flute is played. These holes precisely represent the 7 chakras or the 7 plexuses.

NOW LET US DISCUSS THE MINOR SIDDHIS:

1. The yogi becomes free from hunger and thirst.

2. Freedom from the effects of heat and cold.

3. Freedom from Raga and Dwesha.

    Raga: It is the desire to achieve personal fulfilment.

    Dwesha: A strong feeling of dislike or hostility towards others.

4. Door Darshan: This is known as clairvoyance.

    During the Mahabharata war, Ved Vyasa gave the power of Door Darshan to Sanjay, the charioteer of King Dhritarashtra. The king was blind. So, Sanjay sitting beside him could view and describe all the happenings of the Mahabharata war to Dhritarashtra. So, viewing various incidents from a distance is known as Door Darshan.

5. Door Shravan: Clairaudience: This Siddhi was shown by Lord Krishna in the Mahabharata story. When the Kauravas were undressing Draupadi in the Royal Court of the Kauravas, getting no help from the Pandavas, Draupadi prayed to Lord Krishna. Lord Krishna could listen to her prayer from a distance and supplied an infinitely long saree to her. The wicked brother Duhsasana could not become successful in undressing Draupadi.

6. Mano-Jaya: This is known as the control of one's own mind. Generally, we are slaves of our minds. We act as per our mind. But a yogi works very hard not to obey the directions of the mind. He/ she works as per conscience duly directed by the soul.

7. Kama-rupa: Taking the shape of any living or non-living being. The yogi can take any form – male to a female, female to a male, adult to a child, etc. Yogis, demigods, and some demons have this power. Lord Hanuman was changing His body to look like a monk when He met Lord Rama and His younger brother Lakshman for

the first time in the jungles of Kishkinda. There are many such examples. I have just narrated one.

8. Para-kaya Pravesha:

Anyone who has this Siddhi can enter the body of another person. This is a very risky Siddhi. The yogi should know how to return to his original body. If he fails by chance, then the yogi is bound to stay in the body until its natural death. So, entering into and exiting out of the body techniques should be mastered by the yogi.

Adi Shankar showed such a Siddhi.

In one scriptural debate with the Vedajnya Shree Mandana Mishra, Adishankar defeated him. Mandana Mishra's wife was the judge at that time. Her name was Mata Ubhaya Bharati. She was very knowledgeable in the 4 Vedas. After the defeat of her husband, Mata told Adi Shankar to challenge him in knowledge. Adishankar agreed to the challenge of Mata. Questions concerning knowledge of sex (Rati Vijnana) were asked by Mata during the debate. Adi Shankar was unmarried and very young at that time. He had no knowledge of Rati Vijnana as he was observing Brahmacharya (celibacy). So, he could not answer any of Mata Ubhaya Bharati's questions. He asked for some time to answer her questions. Mata Bharati agreed.

Adi Shankar went to the jungle along with his disciples. They could see that some people were carrying the dead body of the king of that kingdom where Adi Shankar and his disciples were moving around. Adi Shankar decided to enter the body of the dead king. He told his disciples about his proposal. Then, he also told his disciples to guard his dead body, keeping it inside a cave secretly. Whenever they would find that it was not possible to keep the dead body as it is, they were given a mantra by Adi Shankar to remind him to come back to his original body. Accordingly, Adi Shankar entered the dead body of the king. Suddenly, the king was alive, and he woke up. The people felt very happy and took the king to his kingdom. As a king, Adi Shankar enjoyed being with the wives of the king, and in this way, he learned the intricacies of Rati Vijnana. As time passed, the people of the kingdom saw positive changes in their kingdom. The people of the kingdom changed so much that there was no thieving and no natural disasters in the kingdom. The people close to the king, along with the Chief Minister, guessed that some saint must have entered the king's body. Then, the minister ordered his fellowmen to search for dead bodies nearby, and if they found such a body, they were ordered to burn it. This order was known to the followers of Adi Shankar. They recited the mantra and called Adi Shankar back. Adi Shankar immediately left the king's body and entered his own body.

Thereafter, he came to the house of Mandan Mishra and debated with Maa Ubhay Bharati. Adi Shankar defeated Mata. Finally, Adi Shankar won, and Mata became his follower immediately.

This story is a bright example of Para-Kaya Pravesha.

9. Ichchha Mrityu:

This Siddhi allows a person to die at his/her own will and pleasure.

Bhisma, the Paternal Grandfather of the Kuru clan, had the Ichchha Mrityu boon from his mother, Ganga. King Shantanu of Hastinapura and the celestial goddess Ganga (Ganges River) got married because Ganga Mata put a garland on him when he was outside his palace. King Shantanu liked to dress like Lord Shiva. Ganga Mata wanted to marry Lord Shiva. When she saw Shantanu, she could not recognise him as the king of Hastinapura and not Lord Shiva. So, as per the rules, Ganga Mata had to marry Shantanu. Ganga Mata told Shantanu, "I will not stay with you if you scold me." Shantanu agreed to her condition. Ganga Mata gave birth to 6 children. She was killing each newly born baby. Because of the promise, King Shantanu did not scold her, though she committed heinous crimes by killing her newborn babies. Bhisma (Real name Devabrata) was the 7th child. When he was born, Ganga Mata wanted to kill him. Now, Shantanu could not tolerate it further. He scolded Ganga Mata and requested her to leave Bhisma alive. Since King Shantanu scolded her without killing the baby, she went to heaven. Before leaving, King Shantanu asked her, "What will happen to Devabrata without a mother?" Ganga Mata replied, "Let him live or die." This statement of Ganga Mata, bestowed upon Devabrata (name changed to Bhisma afterwards), became a boon to the child. So, Bhisma had the Ichchha Mrityu.

10. Play and meet with the demigods:

A yogi having this Siddhi can play or meet with God or Goddesses. Devarshi Narada has this Siddhi apart from many more siddhis. He has the boon to be Chiranjivi (No death). Whenever he wants to meet or play with God or demigods, he is able to do so. This is the reason Narada can move around all places starting with heaven, Earth, and any Lokas (any level).

11. Yatha Sankalpa:

The accomplished yogis and demigods can do anything based on their wishes.

12. Trikala Jnana:

Saints, yogis, etc., who have this Siddhi know the past, the present, and the future.

13. Vak Siddhi:

What the yogi says, it happens. If the siddha talks to someone, such a thing happens immediately. Many saints and demigods have this power. They can curse or bless as per their own statements. If they tell someone to become some other being, like Rishi, Gautama could convert his wife Ahalya into a stone. Ahalya changed her human form and became a stone.

14. Knowledge of the past life:

Normally, everyone forgets about their past life. But a yogi having this power can clearly know and visualise their past life.

15. The yogi can visualise and learn about all components of the universe, like the knowledge of the stars, planets, and other celestial bodies of various other worlds.

16. Prajna Siddhi:

This Siddhi makes the yogi extremely knowledgeable. His memory power is quite strong, and he has very bright intelligence.

All the above minor siddhis make the yogi great. They can use various siddhis for free.

JNANA AND BHAKTI

By taking the name of Lord Rama near the ears of a person who was dead, he could bring back life to the dead person. Swami Samarth was well known as a Jnana Yogi, whereas Tulsi Das was known as a Bhakti Yogi. In Shrimad Bhagavad Gita, it is clearly stated that there is no difference between Bhakti and Jnana. They are one and the same. Adi Shankar has described that Jnana is the immediate cause of Moksha or Salvation. But while defining Bhakti, he stated that to achieve salvation, Bhakti takes prime importance. Vedantas state that ignorance is the root cause of sorrow. Soon after the veil of ignorance is opened, all sorrows vanish instantly. So, we should treat Bhakti and Jnana as one and the same. Lord Krishna had 16,000 Gopis. All were true devotees of Lord Krishna. All of them were Bhakti yogis. They were able to reach God only by the path of Bhakti. Uddhav, a devotee of Lord Krishna, had an ego that he was a true Jnana Yogi and, thus, a true devotee of God. To make Uddhav realise his folly (Please remember, ego is the root cause of bondage. Ego sprouts because of ignorance), Lord Krishna told him to convey his letter to the Gopis. Uddhav and Lord Krishna were in Mathura, and the Gopis were in Gopa. Upon receiving the orders of Lord Krishna, Uddhav went to Gopa with Lord Krishna's letter. All the Gopis, upon receiving the letter of Lord Krishna, were immersed in the love (Bhakti) of Lord Krishna to the extent that the letter itself was torn. Witnessing this, Uddhav could understand the real nature of Bhakti. After comprehending Bhakti Rasa (the sweet taste of devotion), his ego, which was that of a great devotee of Lord Krishna, was completely eradicated.

There is another story concerning Rukmini and Radha. This story will let you know the real nature of Bhakti or devotion. Basically, Bhakti is a direct connection between the devotee and God or, say, the Soul and the Super Soul.

Please listen to this story carefully.

THE BACKDROP:

Lord Krishna migrated all the people of Mathura to an island in Gujarat state. He established His kingdom there and named it Dwarka. He took this decision because a demon, namely Jarasandha (Father-in-Law) of the earlier slain king Kansa, was creating much trouble for the inhabitants of Mathura. He was waging war against Lord Krishna and Balarama, and because of continuous intermittent wars, the life of the inhabitants of Mathura was extremely unstable and troublesome. Jarasandha was trying to take revenge against Lord Krishna because He killed his son-in-law, the tyrannous king, namely Kansa of Mathura. Kansa was a very wicked king. He was so wicked that he ousted his father from the throne and made him guard the kingdom at night. He was causing lots of trouble for his people, and everyone was very afraid of Kansa. It so happened that during the marriage ceremony of his sister, namely Devaki, he heard a divine message from heaven that the 8th progeny of Devaki would kill him. After listening to this ominous message, he immediately took his sister Devaki and his brother-in-law, namely Vasudeva (Vasudeva was also a good friend of Kansa), to prison. He told Devaki to give all her progenies one by one so that he could kill them, thereby leaving no one to kill him. Lord Krishna was the eighth progeny of Devaki and Vasudeva. This is precisely the reason Kansa, being the real maternal uncle of Lord Krishna, had to be killed. Lord Krishna took birth on Earth to eliminate the demons and ensure peace for the saints and the common people. Later, he encouraged Bhima and gave him the tricks to kill Jarasandha. Finally, the tyrannous demon king Jarasandha of Magadha kingdom was killed. This is the backdrop of why Lord Krishna decided to migrate all his people from Mathura to Dwarka. As usual, Radha, the true devotee of Lord Krishna, was residing in Gopa.

THE MAIN STORY OF RADHA AND RUKMINI:

On one occasion, Radha wanted to visit Lord Krishna in Dwarka. So, she went to Dwarka and met with Lord Krishna. Lord Krishna is also known as Krishna Dwaipayana. Being a king, he had 8 queens known as Ashta Patavansi. Rukmini (Goddess Lakshmi took the incarnation of Rukmini on Earth to be with Lord Krishna) was the head of Ashta Patavansi. Radha spent some time with Lord Krishna and wanted to return to Gopa. Lord

Krishna told Rukmini to give her a glass of milk to drink at the time of her departure. Rukmini did so by giving Radha a glass of hot milk to drink. Radha returned home, leaving Lord Krishna and Dwarka. In the night, when Lord Krishna went to the palace of Rukmini to rest, she wanted to massage Lord Krishna's feet as usual. But lo! There were boils on His feet. Rukmini was feeling very sorry for the wound of Lord Krishna and asked Him how all this happened! Lord Krishna replied, "You gave hot milk to Radha. Because of this, boils came out on my feet." Rukmini was very surprised by these words. She asked, how come You have burns on your feet when Radha drank hot milk? Lord Krishna smiled and said, "The heart of Radha and my feet are joined together. So, when Radha drank the hot milk, my feet were very hot. As a result of this, boils came out. However, please do not worry. I always bear the pains of my devotees and bestow them happiness and peace. By transferring the heat from the heart of Radha, I bestowed her with coolness and peace. Please remember, my devotees are always assured of peace, good health, and prosperity. I bring all the true devotees to my home (Satya Lok)."

This story clearly states that devotion is the path to freedom. The Soul and Super Soul have a lossless joint.

Let me tell you another story: how the Soul and Super Souls joined together.

HANUMAN AND THE CORONATION CEREMONY OF SRI RAMA:

Lord Rama came back to Ayodhya after completing 14 years of banishment. During these 14 years, he killed the demon Ravan and many other demons like Khar, Dushan, Trishira, Kumbhkarn, Meghnad, Anirvan, Mahiravan, etc. Vibhishan, who was a devotee of Lord Rama, became the king of Lanka. He returned in the chariot named Pushpak, which was given to him by Vibhishan so he could return to Ayodhya on time.

Bharat and Shatrughna were the brothers of Lord Rama. They were eagerly waiting for the return of Lord Rama along with the 3 queens, namely Kaushalya, Kaikeyi, and Sumitra. These 3 queens were the consorts of Dashrath, the late king of Ayodhya. Lord Rama was the son of Kaushalya; Bharat was the son of Kaikeyi; Lakshman and Shatrughan were the sons of Sumitra. Lord Rama returned with Sita Mata, his younger brother

Lakshman, Lord Hanuman, Sugriva, Jambavan, Angad, Nal, Nila, and many of his Vanar (Monkey) warriors. The family guru, namely Vasistha, and other great saints such as Jabal, Parashar, Shandilya, etc., were also waiting for the return of Lord Rama to Ayodhya from banishment. All the tenants of Ayodhya were also eagerly waiting for the return of their beloved king, Lord Rama. After the arrival of Lord Rama, His Guru found a suitable date and time for his coronation.

During His most auspicious ceremony, Lord Rama and Sita Mata were sitting on the throne of Ayodhya. On their 2 sides, his brothers Bharat, Lakshman, and Shatrughna were present. Taking a Veer asana pose, Lord Hanuman was sitting just near the feet of Lord Rama and Sita Mata. The coronation function was over with great happiness and joy.

All the brothers, Sugriva, Angad and other Vanars, were very interested in serving their respected Lord Rama and Sita Mata. So, a Seva Chart was made for the newly coronated king. All devotees, starting from Bharat, were feeling jealous of Lord Hanuman. They had a collective feeling that the Lord loved Lord Hanuman very much. So, they wanted to exclude him from the Seva Chart of Lord Rama. On the morrow, everyone was notified to serve Lord Rama as per the Seva Chart. The chart included the Seva timings, starting from the waking up of the Lord till His divine rest at night. Every Sevak, starting from Bharat, went to check his/her own Seva timings. Lord Hanuman was also very inquisitive and eager to know his own slot for Seva. But alas! Lord Hanuman could not see His name on the list. He was fraught with deep sorrow and prayed to Lord Rama to give him a solution so that His name would be included in the Seva Chart. Lo! He got a good solution by the grace of Lord Rama.

WHAT WAS THE SOLUTION?

Lord Hanuman sat near the door from where He could have a vision of the various activities of the Sevakas and Lord Rama. He saw the time when Lord Rama had His divine lunch. Just when He finished eating the divine food, Lord Rama immediately started yawning because He felt sleepy. Exactly at that time, Lord Hanuman, taking the name of Lord Rama, started reciting Sri Rama with a phutki (a sound created at the time of yawning. Usually, we yawn when we feel sleepy. After a good lunch, we usually feel sleepy) by using His right-hand thumb and the middle fingers.

On the first phutki with the name of Sri Rama, Lord Hanuman became quite engrossed in the name of Lord Rama, and as a result, He started making the phutki with the name of Sri Rama continuously without understanding the repercussions thereafter.

The powers of continuous phutki and Japa were so great and intense that Lord Rama could not close His mouth. He was in a state of agape. Everyone was worried. All of them went here and there to find a solution so that Lord Rama would close His mouth. The Ayurvedic doctors were called to take immediate steps. Saints like Vasistha and Jabal were also informed that they needed to find a solution. When nothing happened, finally, all of them endeavoured to have the auspicious presence of Lord Hanuman. Bharat and Lakshman found Lord Hanuman sitting near the outside door and engrossed in reciting Rama Naam rhyming with phutki. It was very astonishing! Lord Hanuman, with His eyes closed, recited Rama Naam with the phutki, which was really a delightful scene. Bharat and Lakshman beseeched Lord Hanuman to stop reciting the Rama mantra Japa along with the phutki. Lord Hanuman immediately stopped the Japa action and was shocked upon hearing about the conditions of Lord Rama. But to the utter astonishment of all, as soon as Lord Hanuman stopped the Japa and phutki, the mouth of Lord Rama was automatically brought back to its original position. Everyone was surprised and asked Lord Hanuman why He took such a step. Lord Hanuman talked about His sorrow for not being allotted a slot to serve Sri Rama. All, including Bharat and Lakshman, felt guilty about their negative action towards Hanuman, the great devotee of Lord Rama, and begged His pardon. But Hanuman felt very sorry because Lord Rama had to undergo such a great punishment owing to His incessant Japa with phutki. He said to all, "When I started the first phutki with the name of my Lord Sri Rama, I was in a trance and I knew nothing thereafter." Everyone was taken aback after listening to the story of Lord Hanuman. They could realise that "There is a direct connection of the Soul and the Super Soul."

Devotees of the Lord have such powers. A true devotee is freed from worldly bondage by the Grace of the Super Soul. All spiritual aspirants should note this and work accordingly.

SOUL (ATMAN)

We are talking a lot about this Atman or the Soul. Let us understand what the characteristics of Atman are.

1. Atman lies fully in the plane of Parama Atman or the Super Soul. If we understand the Universal Theory, then a part, i.e. the soul, in this case, has all the characteristics of the Super Soul. Highly elevated yogis, who have realised themselves and have elevated their souls to the near highest level, who have achieved all the 8 siddhis and the 9 Nidhis, claim that they are God. They profoundly speak out, "Shivoham, Shivoham" – meaning thereby: I am Shuva or the Param Atman!

2. In the Vedas, we have 3 statements. These statements are known as Shruti Shira or the quintessence of the Vedas. These 3 statements are, "Aham Brahmasmi! Prajnanam Brahmam! And Tattwamasi!"

3. Aham Brahmasmi: This means, "I am Brahman; I am the Super Soul."

4. Prajnanam Brahmam: This means, "Super Soul is omniscient."

5. Tattwamasi: It means, "I am That or Thou art That: I (soul) and You (Super Soul) are one and the same."

   Only God-realised souls who are duly elevated and have achieved godhood can say and feel so.

6. When we talk of 'I', there is something which exists in our body as a layer by itself. This is self-effulgent. It has self-intellect, is ever-peaceful, and is filled with joy. It witnesses the 3 states (Jagrat - Awakened State; Swapna - Dream State; and the Sushupti - Dreamless sleep State). We will talk about these 3 states as we proceed. The layer, i.e. 'I', is from our own internalities and is our 'ego'. So very clearly, we can say that the soul is not the ego, neither is it the mind. It is also not the memory nor the intellect. These

4 main internalities are known as 'Antah Karan' - Mana, Buddhi, Ahamkara, and Chitta (mind, intellect, ego, and memory). This soul is also not the 5 sheaths (we will describe these sheaths as we proceed). Our soul is also not the Pancha koshas (these are described later). Our soul has the same characteristics as the soul of all others. This soul remains in all 3 times. The 3 times are Bhuta (the past), Vartman (the present), and Bhavishya (the future).

7. The Atman, being the witness, knows everything during all 3 states. When our intellect is dormant during the dreamless sleep state, Atman knows everything as a witness. It means that even if the body has Pancha koshas, 3 states, Antahkarans, etc., our Atman is completely different from all of these. So, we should not identify ourselves as the body. Rather, we should realise and say, "I am the soul or I am the Atman."

8. This universe is enveloped by the Para Atman, and as we say, Atman is also the Super Soul because every part of the Atman belongs to the Param Atman, so we can also say that Atman envelops the universe. On the contrary, we can also state that no object whatsoever can envelop this Atman. We can say that the effulgence, i.e. the Atman, envelopes all non-effulgence. So Atman only and only illumines the various objects, the stars, the planets, the water, the air, the fire, the ether or Asasa, all living and non-living beings, the metals, and anything that is there in this universe are illumined by the Atman.

9. The Atman has the power to move freely from place to place. This Atman does not abide by anyone or anything. All abide by the Atman. In Purusha Sukta, it is clearly written that "A quarter of it is all the creatures, and the balance three-quarters of this Atman form the divine part in the sky. Not only this, but the Atman is also greater than the Earth, greater than the sky, and it is greater than all these worlds." Everything shines after it shines by itself. That is the Atman. This concept of the infinity of the Atman is clearly stated by the Shrutis, that Atman is Satyam, Anantam, and Jnanam.

- SATYAM: This is the TRUTH. It has no beginning and no end. It does not perish. This is infinite. Here comes the thought of

Maya or Illusion. Maya is also infinite, like Satyam. But it has an end. This is the difference between Maya and Satyam. This is declared by the Vedantas.

- ANANTAM: This is one of the characteristics of the Atman. It is infinite. The universe seems to be infinite; the sky seems to be infinite. The air seems to be infinite. All these are enveloped by the Atman. And hence, all these have limits, whereas the Atman is unlimited and supreme.

- JNANAM: This is knowledge. Atman is Omniscient or all-knowing. All get knowledge from Atman. In Kathopanishad, there is a very nice story about Brahma Jnana or the knowledge by knowing which all other knowledge is known. The source of all knowledge is Brahma Jnana. Let me describe the story of Yama and Nachiketa here as described in Kathopanishad.

BRAHMA VIDYA: IMPARTED TO NACHIKETA BY YAMA RAJ (GOD OF DEATH)

In the ancient days, there was a great sage named Uddalak. He belonged to the Gautam clan. The saints usually perform Yagnas to attain a higher life, leading to immortality or salvation. He had a very brilliant and knowledgeable son. Uddalak knew that his son was the true recipient of Brahma Jnana due to his previous birth. Nachiketa, in his previous incarnation, performed intense penances to attain the sacred knowledge of Brahma Jnana.

Bajashravas Yagna was performed by Saint Uddalak. During the Yagna, as per rules, he donated cows to Brahmins. The quality of the cows was very inferior. The cows were very weak. Some of them were nearing their death due to old age. Looking at this, Nachiketa was very disappointed. Finally, he asked his father, "Dear father, who are you donating to today." At this question, Uddalak felt very angry at the question of his son. Out of great resentment, he said, "I donate you to death." This statement, though made in anger, was a blessing in disguise. With this statement, Nachiketa would go to the Lord of death, Yama Raj, who is a real guru, to teach Brahma Jnana to the real recipient.

When Nachiketa received the orders of his father, he set forth on his journey to the abode of Yama Raj. He reached there, and by that time, Yama Raj was not at his abode. He waited for Lord Yama for 3 days and nights without having any food and water. The consort of Yama requested Nachiketa a lot but to no avail. He replied to her, "Unless or otherwise I meet with Lord Yama, it will amount to disobedience of the orders of my father. So, I must sincerely wait until his return." In earlier times, guests were treated with respect by being given proper food and shelter. But Nachiketa was not prepared to accept any such treatment from anyone other than Yama Raj. After 3 days, Lord Yama returned to his abode. He heard about Nachiketa from his consort and knew that Nachiketa was eagerly waiting for him without receiving any hospitality from her. She also said that Nachiketa looked bright and knowledgeable.

YAMA RAJ:

Yama Raj brought Nachiketa to his palace. He performed due to hospitality for Nachiketa. Thereafter, he said to Nachiketa, "Since you remained hungry for 3 nights, I will give you 3 boons. Otherwise, I will be committing a sin by keeping a saint hungry for 3 nights. Please ask for 3 boons one by one so that my sins can be wiped out. Myself and my family members will receive goodness henceforth."

Nachiketa became quite satisfied listening to Yama Raj's commitment.

The first boon:

Nachiketa said, "Respected Lord of death, my father has become angry with me. Please give me the first boon so that my father will be calm and pacified. He will have no anger against me. Once I get your permission to go back to my father, my father will recognise and accept me."

Yama Raj quickly approved the first boon. Then he asked Nachiketa to state the second boon.

Nachiketa said, "Oh, my dear Lord of death! I know that all the inhabitants of heaven are staying with happiness. No one has any fear. No one becomes old and dies. All maintain their permanent youth. No one in heaven is fraught with thirst and hunger." I very well know that to come to heaven, one should have the 'knowledge of fire.' Only such a person can come to heaven after death. Hence, please give me the 'knowledge of fire' as my second boon from you.

Yama Raj, as promised by him, taught the knowledge of fire to Nachiketa. After saying so, Yama Raj became very happy with Nachiketa and said that as another boon from my side, "I declare that the knowledge of fire that I taught you will be named 'Nachiketin Fire.' Additionally, I am giving you this rosary made of pearls because, after your death, you will come to heaven. In the world, whoever performs this Nachiketin Fire 3 times will come to heaven after death."

KNOWLEDGE OF THE SELF - 3RD BOON FOR NACHIKETA BY YAMA RAJ

Nachiketa was very knowledgeable. He knew that knowledge of the Brahman (Super Soul) was the source of all knowledge. Accordingly, he said, "O Lord of death! There is a doubt lurking in the minds of most of us. Some say that after death, the existence of the soul remains as it is, and others say that after death, the soul does not exist. Your experience about the existence of the soul may kindly be told to me by your kind self. After listening to you, I can clearly understand the real secret of the soul. This is my third boon."

Yama Raj was quite surprised at such a question of erudition. He thought that this concerns the 'knowledge of the self'. Knowledge of the self is not divulged to any person. One needs to understand whether the recipient of such knowledge is deserving or not! So, Yama Raj tried to examine Nachiketa's candidature to impart 'knowledge of the self'.

He said to Nachiketa, "My dear boy, your question is the third boon that I am aware of. I also owe it to you to bestow the third boon. But please withdraw this question and ask me for some other boon. Earlier, many wise demigods debated this question, and they could not find a solution. Please do not coerce me because I promised to bestow you 3 boons."

Then Nachiketa thought for a while and said, "My dear Lord of death! If you say that earlier the demigods could not find an answer to such a question, then it is a very potent one. Who could be the authentic speaker on this other than you to tell me about the state of the soul after death?"

Listening to the replies of Nachiketa, Yama Raj wanted to divert his question by presenting various temptations, such as a big family with 100 children, the provision of many beneficial animals like horses, cows, and elephants, provision of various wealth including gold and golden ornaments; becoming an emperor of the largest kingdom on Earth, etc.

Again, he also told him to ask for as many years of life on Earth as possible to enjoy the various luxuries he had promised.

Nachiketa listened to all these temptations, but he was unperturbed and fearless. Looking at this, Yama Raj offered him the luxuries of heaven like a chariot, divine angels, and damsels, etc. He also added that many saints vie for these luxuries but are not able to get them.

Nachiketa thought that all these luxurious things were not at all comparable with the 'knowledge of the self.' He said, "My dear Lord of death, all these are temporary. They may remain or get destroyed before a Kalpa (4.32 billion years is the duration of a Kalpa). They do not provide real happiness. We get sorrows by having this wealth, family members, angels, etc. This is also very clearly stated in the Bhagavad Gita chapter 5, stanza 22. All the temporary happiness not only gives sorrows and pain but reduces the power of our sense organs and destroys our own Dharma. Even Brahma must meet his death. So please keep all these chariots, angels, golden ornaments, horses, cows, etc. with you. I do not need all these."

He further stated, "Human beings can never be satisfied with wealth. As fire clarifies butter, it increases its intensity; similarly, all luxury-giving items can never satisfy our desires. Rather, such provision increases our desires and keeps us tethered. In my view, no intellectuals ask for riches and luxuries that cause us suffering. Whatever riches are needed to lead my life are already available to me after getting your divine vision. A long life is there until we have control over our death. But the control eventually loosens. I do not want all these. Nothing is superior to 'the knowledge of the self.' And hence, please impart to me 'knowledge of the self.' This is my prayer to you."

Note: Just see the confidence of Nachiketa. He knew well that 'knowledge of the self' is the ultimate. This knowledge bestows freedom. Nachiketa was very decisive in learning this knowledge.

After listening to the confident, fearless, and decisive replies from Nachiketa, Yama Raj was very pleased. He started imparting 'the knowledge of self' in the following manner:

Yama Raj said, "The human birth is unlike the birth of other animals and living organisms. All others except human beings are subject to get the results as per their karma (action). In this birth, the human being is to enquire into the self to get a better life in the future. This is broadly divided into 2 parts: Sreyas and Preyas."

SHREYAS: This is a method by which one can live without pain and suffering. The other objective of this method is to be one with the all-blissful Param Atman.

PREYAS: This is a method by which the human being gets a family (wife, children, etc.), wealth, fixed assets, fame, respect in society, and various sources of articles that give temporary pleasure and joy.

Both methods are very powerful and attract human beings throughout their lifetime.

Many people need immediate happiness and luxury. They do not think of the aftermath of accepting these life leading methods. This is the reason they get strongly attracted to Preyas.

Very few, due to the blessings of God, understand that luxury, riches, acquiring a family, and the like lead to pain and suffering. Owing to the undesirable results of the Preyas methodology, they develop a dispassion towards this. Hence, they make all-out efforts very sincerely to adopt the Shreyas.

Of these 2 types of people, those who adhere to the Shreyas methodology receive the blessings of God and always enjoy goodness in their lifetime. Eventually, through their persistent efforts, they become freed from the bondage of life (the repeated birth and death cycle) and elevate themselves to Satyaloka, the realm of God.

The folks who adopt Preyas never get everlasting peace. Whatever state of happiness they feel is illusory. On the contrary, all the temporary luxury and happiness turn out to be a deep sorrow for these people, and they never get freedom from the bondage of the world. They fully deviate from true happiness. As the taste of the neem leaf is very bitter but helps heal many diseases, in the same manner, Shreyas may be very difficult to adopt. But it gives ultimate peace, happiness, and everlasting joy. On the contrary, it is like sweets. Just as a person ultimately gets sorrows by consuming too many sweets, in the same way, the persons accepting the path of Prayas get sorrows, pains, and suffering.

Many people do not believe in reincarnation. They think that there is only one birth. So, they go on the path of Preyas to seek temporary pleasure and happiness. Eventually, they succumb to various diseases, extreme distress, etc.

The persons who understand water in milk and drink the milk from the solution like that of a swan become very successful in this life and get the blessings of God. All persons devoid of conscience opt for the path of Preyas. Yogakshema is the assurance given by God for the belongings of human beings when they surrender unto Him. All people with low knowledge beseech God to protect their various assets and ask God for more and more. However, the wise and the erudite believe in dispassion. He/she does not expect anything from God. He is well disposed by his own decisions to go on the path of Shreyas to get permanent peace and finally mingle with God. By saying so, Yama Raj is clearly indicating that Nachiketa has a strong dispassion against belongings and worldly pleasure.

VIDYA AND AVIDYA

Vidya and Avidya are like light and darkness. They give results differently. A person who is inclined towards a luxurious lifestyle can never progress in life's welfare. People who want the welfare of their lives never pay any attention to luxurious living. Yama Raj said, "O Nachiketa, you have a good likeness to acquire true knowledge. This is because you have shunned all forms of luxuries, and you do not have an iota of temptation toward worldly comforts."

"A blind, when guided by another blind, can never reach their destination. They get away from their target. Since they have lost their path, they either fall into a deep hole or get pricked by thorns lying on their way. They may dash against some walls or could be attacked by animals. Such fools take birth in the lower and sorrowful wombs like animals, birds, worms, insects, etc., and they verily enter the realm of darkness or the realm of the dungeon for an infinite period and suffer from various pains."

"Persons who think themselves to be very wise and possess such ego that they do not even care for the sayings of the great seers, ignore their advice and run after matters giving temporary pleasure and happiness. Though they have the rare body of a human being, still, owing to the above, they waste their valuable life."

"In this way, the unwise get attracted to the luxuries of life and get trapped. They do not find time to take the name of God. They are not able to discriminate between dharma and adharma. They verily commit adharma because the temptation of luxurious living leads them to dangerous propositions of managing their lives. They never think of later life. They think that the present life is everything for them. Their Antahkaran never alerts them about the dangers of having indulged in wealth, family, and such temporary comforts, which ultimately cause pain and suffering. They never believe in heaven, in the dungeon. They only think about the place where they exist and have no vision of the higher details of the universe. Because of this ignorance (Avidya), they become bound to move from womb to womb and have repeated births and deaths. Freedom becomes a dream for them."

Yama Raj said, "The persons who have realised their souls are very rare. Strong believers in worldly activities never believe in God, who is present everywhere and in our hearts. It is not that easy to get 'knowledge of the self'. This knowledge is also not very common. You may not hear about this knowledge from most people. People only discuss subjects and get involved in those that bind us and give us diseases, pains, and suffering. From the time they wake up until they rest at night, they only talk about worldly affairs. Even if they hear about 'knowledge of the self' from somewhere, they have little time to reflect and meditate on it. Many people like to listen to and ponder this subject. However, due to their burdensome activities or their own ignorance, they do not pursue the path to achieve freedom and God's realisation. A person who can clearly discuss 'knowledge of the self or Atma Jnana' and make the listeners and aspirants understand the concept, process, etc., Brahma Vidya (knowledge of the self) is rare. So, we have seen that both are rarely available. When a person clearly listens about Atma Jnana, through continuous meditation, eventually, he/she gains the 'knowledge of the self' and becomes free in this and future lives."

Now please listen about this Atma Tattva or Brahma Vidya, said Yama Raj to Nachiketa. He said, "Whatever subtle material is there, still subtler is this Atma Tatva. The subject matter is so esoteric and deep that until a person who is the knower of the self is available, it is very difficult to enter the realm of Atma Tattva. If a person has less knowledge, if he imparts the Atma Jnana, then the practitioner of the aspirant cannot become successful. Again, it is not easy to comprehend Atma Jnana. Even if a person does not listen to anyone analyse this, Atma Tattva will still not be able to understand it. Hence, it is necessary that the aspirant fully listen to Atma Jnana or Atma Tattva. The speaker should have the right knowledge and a seer. Only then will he/she be able to speak and make the listener understand the theory and practices of Atma Jnana. Again, one should understand that this knowledge is beyond all arguments."

Yama Raj was praising Nachiketa, addressing him as "Oh, my dear disciple! I am very pleased with your pure mind and sincerity. No one can get this sincerity from arguing. Such great sincerity can only be possible if there are the blessings of God and great seers. Such sincerity encourages the aspirant to work towards getting Atma Jnana. After giving so much worldly temptation to you, your determination did not deviate. From all these symptoms, it is now clear that you are an ideal being. 'Oh, my dear Nachiketa,' I am always interested in getting sincere disciples like you who have the ardent interest to inquire into the self."

YAMA RAJ TALKS ABOUT THE STATE OF 'DESIRELESSNESS'

Yama Raj now talks to Nachiketa about the benefits of the state of 'desirelessness'. He said, "The result of various activities may be very great. It might produce very high worth in terms of money and materials. But one day, all these will come to an end. Hence, all these are unreal and transitory in nature. Again, it is also true that efforts towards the achievement of the unreal can never get the real. Though, on your request, as a second boon to you, I talked about the process and practicability of Nachiket Fire; I told you it was a matter of duty. The results of all these activities do not lead to the real or to God. The importance of the state of desirelessness is that I could get the all-dutiful Param Atman by worshipping Him with the various worldly materials without having an iota of expectation or any amount of desire."

In Shrimad Bhagavad Gita, it is stated that the knower of all the 4 Vedas performs havan (putting clarified butter and other articles of Yagna in the sacred fire) by the articles prescribed in the Vedas without any desire. They perform the activities called Brahm Arpan (offering to Brahman) through the sacred fire, namely Ahavaniya (the name of a sacred fire prescribed in the Vedas). These sacred performances for God without having an iota of desire lead them to Brahman after their demise. They get freed from the cycles of birth and death. So, all who are aspiring for liberation (in Sanskrit, they are called 'Mumukshu') should not leave karma or work/activities. So in the Vedas, wherever it is stated to leave karma/ work, understand, leave the results of karma/work and do not leave karma/work.

Yama Raj wanted to praise Nachiketa further by saying, "I have seen the state of desirelessness in you in its complete form. You have the best wisdom and are devoid of all wishes. Though I offered you all the luxuries of heaven, you still did not want all this transitory wealth. You wanted to learn the Brahma Vidya (Atma Jnana) from me without keeping any other desire. It is not common. This is why I agree that you have a sharp intellect, are non-attached, and deserve to get the most esoteric knowledge of Brahma Vidya."

Now, Yama Raj wanted to create the power of enquiry into the Antahkaran (mind, intellect, ego, and memory) of Nachiketa of the philosophy of Brahman. He told him as described below. Please read and reflect on the following 2 statements carefully:

- This whole universe is like an unreal dense forest. But all this universe is pervaded by Brahman. He is omnipresent and is present in the cave of the heart of each and everyone.

- Though Brahman is present everywhere, He is enveloped by the cover of Yogamaya (the illusive power of the Lord/ Brahman). All our Indriyas (Sensory and motor nerves) cannot see nor touch the Brahman because He is secretly seated within the core of our heart. Spiritual aspirants with pure intellect, fortitude, erudition who hold their minds and intellect on the immaculate Brahman without wavering can attain Him. These Yogis achieve the state of non-duality such as happiness and sorrowfulness permanently.

The yogi or the spiritual aspirant should listen to this advice with due love and respect from a guru or an Atma Jnani. After listening to all these, he/she should reflect upon all the statements. Then he needs to analyse with the help of his intellect and apply his own mind to the various statements told by the guru. By doing this, when the person gains Atma Jnana, from that moment he attains Param Brahman Param Atman. Then he becomes fully absorbed in the ocean of happiness. "Oh! My dear Nachiketa, the door to Param Dham is open for you. No one can restrict you from entering the Satya Loka. You deserve to receive the knowledge of the Brahman. I fully agree with this," said Yama Raj.

After listening to the greatness of Param Brahma Purushottama and knowing that he deserves to receive Brahma Jnana, the anxiety to know about the Brahman grew in the minds of Nachiketa. After listening to all the praises from Yama Raj, he was also feeling quite humbled with due honesty. Then he said to Yama Raj, "Oh my dear Guru, if you are so much pleased with me, then please tell me about the philosophies of the Brahman which are beyond the times (past, present, future), beyond the cause and its effect, and beyond all Dharma and Adharma. Dharma is the base on which everything is hinged upon, and adharma is just its opposite. For example, Truth is Dharma and False is Adharma. Truth is infinite and has no end. False or Maya or Illusion is infinite, but it has a definite end."

Listening to the question on the philosophies of the Brahman, Yama Raj, having promised to explain the knowledge of Brahman, the supreme of all knowledge, started talking about the letter OM and its significance. He said, "All the Vedas in various stanzas have duly signified the letter 'OM.' OM is the supreme objective of all austerities and spiritual practices (Sadhana). To get to the proximity and the true knowledge of OM, the Sadhaka (the spiritual aspirant) must resort to celibacy (Brahmacharya), Vanaprastha (in later life towards old age, worldly persons go to the forest and live there to perform Sadhana) and sannyasa (asceticism) with sincerity and due devotion to spiritual achievement. I am now explaining to you in gist, the philosophies of the same Purushottama. He is OM, this one letter."

Purushottama has no name. Still, we call Him by many names. Of all the names of the Brahman, it is agreed that 'OM' is supreme. So, there is no difference between the name OM and the Brahman. Speaking thus, Yama Raj said, "'OM' is Pranav, 'OM' substitutes Purushottama. Omkar is Brahman, and Omkar is Param Purusha. So, both Brahman and Param Brahman are known as 'OM'. This philosophy must be well understood by the Sadhaka and can choose any one of the 2. It is because both are one and the same. They are inseparable."

To get Param Brahman, the only source is 'OM.' Hence 'OM' is to be practised by the Sadhakas by all means. There is no other process to get the divine shelter of the Brahman. OM is the only invincible weapon to get God and thereby to attain liberation (freedom from the bondage). Any Sadhak who understands this secret and fully depends on 'OM' with love and devotion, he/she gets the supreme fame of attaining salvation. By this way, stating OM as the symbol of Brahma and Param Brahman, Yama Raj started to talk about the characteristics of the SOUL (Atman).

SOUL (ATMA) EXPLAINED

Yama Raj is explaining the purity and deathless characteristics of Atma. Because, until the Sadhaka has not realised their own deathlessness and fearlessness, and until they have not understood the difference between transitory objects like the body, materials, etc., they will not have dispassion. They will not have the yearning for liberation from the very core of the heart and from the Antahkarans (mind, intellect, ego, and memory). They should have a strong faith that Atman is Sat-Chit-Anand. Sat has no death or untruth. Chit is knowledge. Anand is bliss. Hence, we say Satchidananda is the qualities of the Atman. The Sadhaka has no relationship with:

- the Illusion which is transitory

- that, which has an end

- the various comforts and luxuries.

The Sadhaka has neither a beginning nor an end. They are infinite. They have neither any causes nor anything to perform. And hence, they are not bound by birth and death, have one taste, and are fearless. They do not die with the death of the body.

A person who thinks this Atman is subject to death or accepts that the Atman is subject to death; he/she is unaware of the characteristics of the Atman and is in delusion. Do not take cognition of their words or opinions. In fact, Atma does not kill anyone nor can Atman be killed by anyone. The body is to be considered a thing of enjoyment and is subject to death, while Atman is to be considered constant or true. Atman does not change. So, considering all this and giving up this transitory body, one should be with the Atman, the changeless and ever-blissful. All Sadhakas should treat the enjoyment of the body as non-permanent, causing sorrow and pain, and take shelter of the Param Atman or Param Brahman by merging the soul with the Super Soul.

SUPER SOUL: PARAM ATMAN

Thus, describing the characteristics of the soul (Atman), Yama Raj could create in Nachiketa's Antahkarans and yearning to know Purushottama or the Super Soul. And then he started discourses on the Super Soul or Purushottama.

It was told earlier that soul is pure. Here, the soul is named 'Jantu' and it is said to have attained its old age. The significance of old age is stated here;

The soul also resides in the cave of our heart near the Super Soul. Though the Super Soul can know everything of the soul, still the soul is not looking at the Super Soul, even if they are very near. Rather, the soul is wasting its own time like the other lower creatures (animals, birds, insects, etc.) and is very much attached to the body. This is precisely the reason why the soul is said to be in a state of old age. The yogis, who after duly understanding the ill effects of this transitory body and the various luxuries, verily seek the Supreme, who is not within the luxuries and not within the transitory. The Sadhaka understands that the Super Soul is smaller than the smallest element and larger than the largest elements. He/she has become calm and unattached from the worldly activities, which are treated as duties in the Vedas. He/she verily receives the blessings of the Brahman (the Super Soul). After winning over the Indriyas (sense organs) and with the purity of the intellect and happiness, he/she meditates upon God and becomes a part of the Supreme Bliss.

He is Achintya, which means we cannot even think of the Brahman. Because of this reason, He takes the shape of an object smaller than the smallest and at the same time can also take the shape of an object bigger than the biggest. It is quite interesting to think about the Brahman (beyond all thoughts, and the source of the dual being only ONE). Purushottama resides in Satya Loka, but if His true devotee remembers Him and calls Him, then He leaves His Satya Lok and can travel from a distance to very remote places with ease and a speed much better than the speed of the mind. He is such that even if he is sleeping at His place, on the call of His ardent devotee, He is there owing to His omnipresence characteristics. He has no ego, even if He has everything, all powers, all knowledge, etc. Yama Raj is saying, "Who other than me can recognise the real deserving spiritual aspirant to know the Param Atman, the Super Soul, the Brahman."

CHARACTERISTICS OF DEVOTEES WHO KNOW THE LORD'S GREATNESS

We know that our body is temporary and it undergoes various changes when the body is active right from birth till death. Param Atman stays in the body and it has no shape. It is not physically existing exactly like the Atman. Owing to this reason, God is constant and immobile. God is completely different from nature, the place, and time. He is independent of all these. He is great and all-pervasive. The wise, once knowing the Brahman like this, do not lament whatsoever. This is the sign of the wise who understands the greatness of God.

Who can attain Param Atma?

It is very difficult for a yogi who performs Purushartha (performance to elevate one's own soul) to get God or the Param Brahman. But it is very possible for the wise to get God, if and only if God chooses the yogi.

Yama Raj said to Nachiketa, "This Parameshwar Paramatma is not available to the people who do Pravachan (talk about God and spirituality). He is not available to the people who clearly state about God after going through the Vedas and other scriptures. God is also not available through logical reasoning. Similarly, God is not available to those who inflate themselves out of ego and debate about God thinking that they know everything. God is also not available to those who spend much of their time listening to the various stories of God. But whom God chooses by Himself, he/she only gets God (Param Atma Parameshwar). These people have an ardent and very deep desire to get God. All these devotees who are chosen by God cannot live without God. They never depend on their Spiritual Sadhana and Intelligence. They wait eagerly for the mercy of God. For such devotees, God uncovers the veil of Yog maya (The illusive or maya power of God)."

People who can understand God:

Yama Raj describes here the people who can get to God.

Persons, after studying the Vedas and various scriptures thoroughly, and after listening to the knowledge of the Brahman from the wise and the erudite, will not be able to find God if:

- their Antahkarans (mind, intellect, ego, and memory) are tethered by the ropes of various worldly desires

- They have not left their wicked nature.

- their minds are not at peace because they do not believe in God

- Not controlling the Indriyas, mind, and the intellect

Even if these individuals meditate on God using their intellect, owing to the aforementioned natures, they cannot love the infinite mercy of God. On the contrary, they truly neglect God. Due to these reasons, they do not deserve to receive the mercy of God.

JIVATMA AND PARAMATMA (JIVA AND BRAHMA)

This human body is rare. This is proclaimed by the wise who have duly studied all the 4 Vedas and other scriptures. Also, this is agreed by the positive-minded devotees of the Lord who perform havan (sacrificial fire) as prescribed by the Vedas. Due to the good work done by the Jivatma in the past birth, God has become very merciful and given the Jivatma the rare human birth. This is because, by getting this body, the Jiva will take on spiritual Sadhana for Soul Elevation. And not only that, to help the Jiva, God (Param Atma) resides in the heart of the person where is the seat of the Jivatma. From this one can well understand how God is very merciful and has the interest to take the Jivatma to Satya Loka, the abode of permanent peace. There is no death there and once Jivatma enters the realm of Satya Lok, there is no return of the Jivatma to the world full of bondage, pain, and sorrow. Both Jivatma and Param Atma stay together in the heart of the human being and observe the maintenance of truth. There is a difference here. Jivatma must enjoy the fruits of good and bad karmas. Whereas, Param Atma remains as a witness near the Jivatma and ensures that Jivatma enjoys the fruits of the various karmas (actions). By the cooperation of these 2, all the works in the world are performed. Jivatma gets happiness when He goes to the Brahman or the Param Atma. Everyone goes to the person who bestows happiness. If there is no difference between the Jivatma (Jivatma is special, constant, having low knowledge and an enjoyer of the fruits of both happiness and sorrowfulness) from the Param Atma, then there would have been no difference between light and darkness. You can think of the Param Atma who makes Jivatma drink the truth and Jivatma drinks the truth. This way remaining side by side they are different like the brightness and the shadow. Like the shadow, Jivatma has low illumination and has low knowledge. Whereas Param Atma is fully bright and omniscient like that of the sunshine. Jivatma sits on the chariot, the body. This Param Atman always wants to get Jivatma who sits in the same body and very near to Him. So Jivatma need not have to go to various places far or near to get Param Atma. From these statements, one can clearly understand that both Jivatma and Param Atma are different and not one and the same.

After realising this secret, the human being should not have any ego of powers and capabilities. He should not feel proud of anything. Rather, he should think of Param Purush who is seated in his heart of hearts.

PRAYER TO GOD TO KNOW HIM:

The first and foremost Spiritual Sadhana process is to be known by the aspirant. And to perform this process, we should have energy and capability. To get all this, we need to pray to the Param Atman.

Yama Raj says, "Pray to the God, O Param Atman! Please give us capabilities so that we will know the processes involved in performing auspicious rites like Yagna without having an iota of desire. By performing Yagna, we will obey your orders and feel happy. The state of fearlessness be bestowed on all the devotees who are interested in knowing thyself, who is constant having no beginning and no end."

After speaking thus, Yama Raj now says:

As we construct bridges to cross water bodies, in the same manner to cross this sorrowful and painful world of bondage, all spiritual aspirants (Sadhakas) by controlling the Indriyas (sense organs) should work towards the welfare of one's own soul. Persons who work under the guidance or to fulfil one's own attachment, anger, and greed etc. cannot take part in the welfare of the world. As per Shrimad Bhagavad Gita, the friend of the Atman is the Atman itself. One must make all-out efforts to have the knowledge of the soul and hence the knowledge of the Super Soul. If we must be free from worldly bondages, then we must work towards acquiring the knowledge of the Brahman. The Sadhakas should control the senses and by doing so, they can increase their own capabilities to know God.

ATMAN GOT SEPARATED FROM PARAMATMAN

This Atman, which was earlier with the Param Atman, has come from its source, the Param Atman, and thereafter is moving from womb to womb in various worlds. Our Earth is one among the myriads of worlds in this universe. This Atman, after being out of its own source, is searching for happiness hither and thither. The Atman is feeling restless in various wombs and then in various bodies but has no peace anywhere till at length it reaches the Param Atman, which is its real home, one can say. But the Param Atman is very kind. After seeing the constant distress of the Atman, He provides a body so that it can reside there and can perform spiritual Sadhana while in this body to elevate its own soul and come back to its own abode, i.e. Satya Loka. This body is known as the 'chariot.' Again, God has provided the various sense organs (Indriyas). These sense organs are very powerful and are compared to horses. The Indriyas or the horses of the chariot are to be controlled or else they will run berserk. To bridle these strong horses, God has given the mind. So, our mind is the bridle that can control the movement of the horses. Our intellect is the charioteer. Atman is seated in this chariot. So, Atman is the owner of the entire body. Now this Atman is expected to inspire the intellect to listen, reflect, and meditate (Shravan, Manan, Nididhyasana) upon the powers, the abode, and activities of the Param Atman. By doing these 3 easy means slowly, the Atman will again come back to the abode of the Param Atman, which is known as Satya Loka.

ATMAN IS NOT DOING ITS OWN DUTIES:

Though Param Atman being so kind has given intellect to the body, still the Atman has not done its prime duties to inspire the intellect as desired. This is because the Atman is very much attached to the body. As a result of this, the intellect has become very careless. The mind, which is working as the bridle, and the sense organs, which are working as the horses for the body or the chariot, are now having no control of the intellect, so they are set free to perform as per their own wishes. So, what is now happening to the Atman:

The Atman is experiencing various happinesses and sorrows while fully involved in worldly affairs along with the mind and the Indriyas. Basically, if the Atman had no body, it would not have experienced happiness and sorrow. However, worldly happiness is not permanent. Similarly, sorrows are also not permanent. Both fluctuate with the passage of time. Essentially, under the influence of happiness and sorrow, the Atman is in a state of restlessness. It must endure and tolerate situations that are transitory in nature. Without a body, the Atman cannot satisfy its own desires. In other words, without the body, the Atman would never be able to fulfil its own desires.

WHY THE INDRIYAS FOLLOW
THE PATH OF WORLDLY ACTIVITIES

As such, we have seen that the Indriyas are not turning towards the Param Atman. What could be the reasons? Let us understand this:

It is known that in any chariot, if the charioteer correctly applies the bridle on the horses, then the horses will be bound to trace the proper path. Here the proper path means the path or the processes involved in spiritual Sadhana to get permanent freedom from this world. But this is not happening here because the intellect is not doing as per the directives of the conscience. The horses like to speedily go to places where they can get green grass to eat. These green grasses can be compared to the worldly pleasures. The skin wants a good touch, the tongue wants a good taste, the eyes want to see beautiful objects, our ears want to listen to melodious music, and our nose wants to smell nice fragrances to get happiness and pleasure. But what is our objective? To go back to our own permanent residence, which is the abode of the Param Atman. So the intellect has to be strong and decisive. It should act as per our conscience. Then only the mind and the Indriyas will be under the control of the intellect. Since the Atman has the conscience and it does not work properly. As a result of this, instead of controlling the mind and the Indriyas, it gets controlled by them. All the horses along with the mind drag the chariot to deep holes where the chariot falls. It is already understood that the horses are very powerful and they are also very wicked. This is precisely the reason; the Atman is in permanent distress.

It is now understood that if the Atman works as per the conscience and directs the intellect accordingly without having attachment to the worldly activities (through sense pleasures etc.), then the mind, which is the bridle, can control the strong and the wicked horses who are the 10 Indriyas (5 Karmendriya and 5 Jnanendriya as discussed earlier), and then only all these will have the right approach to listen, reflect, and meditate upon God.

Whose intellect does not abide by the conscience and works outside the realms of performing proper duties, such an intellect remains under the mind. And what is this mind! It makes and breaks the various desires and is not stable. All entities having desires thus pollute the basic pure thoughts. These polluted thoughts verily engross the various Indriyas to perform undesirable activities. So only, our intellect becomes weak and fully becomes a slave of the sense organs. Owing to these reasons, being in the body by the grace of God, the Atman does not get the Supreme state. Since God has given us the human body, we are supposed to fulfil His desires by resorting to Spiritual Sadhana without becoming the slaves of the minds and the various Indriyas. The intellect when duly abides by the conscience, the mind becomes fully controlled. Then only the sense organs will be able to perform various activities as ordained by God without having any desires. In this state, the human being is rightly resolved. He/she remains away from anger, greed, attachment, and the likes. Such a human being conducts all his works which make him/her divine and finally these human beings get their soul duly elevated and eventually, they reach the abode of Param Atman. These freed souls achieve permanent freedom. Being in Satya Loka, these elevated human beings never return to the world and never fall into the unending cycles of birth and death.

After obtaining this rare human body owing to the grace of God, we must try our level best to seek the Supreme goal. We should engage our minds to understand and think about the philosophies of God. We should engage our speech faculty in reciting the qualities of God. Our eyes should be fully engaged to view the divine appearance of God in some form other (yogis view God through their internal eyes and others view God in the various forms). Similarly, we should engage our ears to listen to the various prayers meant for God. This way we can purify our Indriyas. God's name should taste very sweet to us, God's name should be very melodious for us, God's various forms should be creating gratefulness and the all-merciful qualities of God in our Antahkaran. We should do work so that our body stays healthy. All the work performed by us should have no anticipations. This is the state of desirelessness. We are not supposed to claim ownership of the activities done by us. All the works are to be offered to God. God has the sole authority to bestow the results of all the activities accomplished by us. This is the state of being divine and by doing like this the human beings are said to be doing their duties as per the orders of Param Atman. Our works, thoughts, sense organs are made pure and divine by this. This is the basic objective of God when He put our Atman in this rare human body. So, we should remain ever grateful to Him and work towards elevating our own souls.

REFRAINING FROM THE INDRIYAS INVOLVEMENT IN UNDESIRABLE ACTIONS:

Since our duties are to refrain from the Indriyas (sense organs) from engaging in undesirable activities and instead deploying them in the path of achieving divinity, it is a very difficult task. We need to know the basic philosophies and methods of how to prevent the Indriyas from engaging in activities that are not in line with the wishes of God.

Wealth and the various worldly objects are very strong and have great attractive power. The Sadhakas get easily attracted by these powerful forces. So, what is to be done!

The Sadhakas are to keep themselves fully isolated from these attractive forces such as objects giving worldly pleasures. Our minds are stronger than these worldly attractions like wealth, luxury-giving objects, etc. Intellect is still stronger than the mind. Our intellect can quell the mental vibrations such as anger, greed, attachment, and the like. If due to the influence of our intellect, our minds do not get attracted to the worldly wealth and objects, then the Indriyas will become powerless. They will not become berserk or wayward. So basically, human beings should understand and duly realise the infinite powers of our souls, and if such is done, then the minds, Indriyas are bound to obey the directives of our intellect. We should always understand that our soul (Atman or the Jivatma) is great. We must realise this.

We have gross Indriyas which have their respective orbs in our brain. These orbs give powers to the various Indriyas. These Indriyas are created from the Pancha Bhutas (Kshiti, Aap, Tej, Marut and Vyom). The nose is created from Kshiti or the Earth material. The tongue is created from Aap or water. The eye is created from fire. The skin is created from Marut or Vayu (air). Shrotra or the power of listening is created from Vyom or Ether. The Indriyas have the qualities of the various Bhutas as described above. For example, our eyes receive the qualities of fire. These qualities are not received by the power of listening or, for that matter, the power of smell. According to these basic rules, the Indriyas receive the senses accordingly. All have different qualities. The causes are always finer than the work. Why do we work? It is because someone has insisted on us doing so. So, the controller is the basic cause. When we see something or hear anything, we act accordingly. The trigger comes from the sense organs externally, but internally, the respective orbs sense and thereby the intellect understands and orders the respective Indriyas to respond. The Indriyas do not act suo moto. So, we say that the intellect is the strongest of all. Once it abides and works as per the conscience, which is the directives of the Atman, then all our activities become divine. The mind is subtler than the Indriyas. The well-resolved and decisive intellect is subtler than the mind. The Mahat Tatva, which is the conscience and the quality of the Atman, is subtler than the intellect. In this way, the spiritual aspirant, through due analysis and understanding of the subtle to the subtler to the subtlest, performs the processes for achieving Soul Elevation and ultimately gets liberated.

WHAT IS TRIGUNA AND WHAT IS AVYAKTA?

The 3 Gunas, that is the 3 modes such as the mode of goodness, calmness, and harmony (Sattva); the mode of passion, activity, and movement (Rajas); and the mode of ignorance, inertia, or laziness (Tamas), are known as the trigunas. We operate under the influence of these 3 Gunas. When we operate in Sattva Guna, we always think good, do good, and do not expect any return from our activities. We are very pure in our body, mind, and speech (Kaya, Mana, and Vakya). In the mode of Rajas, we work and perform all duties and activities, but we expect a return from our activities. So, in our body, mind, and speech; whatever we do, whomever we talk to or interact with, we always think of some return. This way Rajas is dominant in us. Tamas is the lowest of all the modes. People who are lazy and people who want to benefit from others without doing any activities operate in this mode. They are very ignorant about the body, mind, and speech faculties. They never improve in their lives. They bring sorrows and pains to others, even to their own relatives. Whereas God is beyond all the Gunas. So, He is termed as Triguna Rahita.

Now let us discuss Avyakta: Avyakta means one who is not visible or not revealed. In the Gita, this quality is stated as 'Doorataya or Ati Dustara.' We have mentioned that Param Atman stays very near to the Atman, but due to the 'Veil of Illusion or Maya,' He is not visible to the Atman. The Atman must work towards elevating itself. No one other than the Atman must perform Purushartha so that it can elevate its own soul. Only then will the Veil of Illusion be lifted by God, and He will be clearly visible to the Atman. Therefore, when we say that Param Atman is more powerful than the Atman, it is evident. The Atman has all rights over the intellect, the mind, the memory, and the various Indriyas. The Atman must guide all the subordinates to turn towards God and always contemplate God. This Avyakta or maya remains between God and the Atman. Maya is more powerful than the Atman. In reality, maya is the illusive power of God. God is all-powerful and all-knowing. Therefore, only when God desires the Atman to see Him, does He remove the maya and reveal Himself to the Atman. The Atman has only one solution, and that is to 'surrender to God.'

GOD IS THE SOURCE OF ALL SOURCES:

Look, as we understand from the subtle argument, we can say that the mind is subtler than the Indriyas, the intellect is subtler than the mind, the conscience, which is the power of the Atman, is subtler than the intellect, maya is subtler than the Atman, and finally, Param Atman is subtler than maya. The source can also be understood through this argument. Earth is the source of the Body or Ghata, water is the source of the Earth, fire is the source of water, air is the source of fire, and finally, God or Param Atman is the source of all. So, 'God is the Source of all Sources.'

GOD IS THE KNOWER OF EVERYTHING:

God, being omniscient, is seated in the hearts of everything that is under His own creation. To know Him or, for that matter, to see Him, one needs to have the eye of their own intellect. This eye can only be opened provided the subject or the aspirant performs spiritual Sadhana and makes themselves a deserving candidate for the elevation of the soul. When the aspirant becomes deserving to know God, the cover of maya will be automatically uncovered, and everything becomes clear. You can take the example of the Sun, which is covered by the cloud on a rainy day. As soon as the clouds move away from the Sun, we can see brightness or the daylight. The Sun is very clearly visible to us. Similarly, when the maya disappears, God is visible and brightens the intellect of the yogi.

THE DESERVING ASPIRANT TO KNOW GOD;

Whose mind is under the control of the Indriyas, whose intellectual power is within the scope of the external world, such an aspirant cannot find God even if he/she searches for God in all the worlds of this universe. But on the contrary, if the aspirant has controlled the Indriyas and the mind and clearly obeys the ubiquitousness of God in all beings, he/she becomes a deserving candidate to realise God. These aspirants can pacify their minds by redirecting the Indriyas towards the analysis of the subtle, the subtler, and the subtlest, i.e. the Param Atman, and put all their efforts with deep concentration on the existence of God in their bodies. Such aspirants can realise God.

RETRACEMENT PROCESS TO BE WITH GOD:

This process, though it seems difficult at the outset, as the aspirant practices, his/her resolve becomes stronger, and this way, getting closer to God eventually becomes possible. Initially, retract the Indriyas to be fully absorbed in the mind. It is as if the Indriyas have truly surrendered to the mind. The speech faculty is not talking, the listening faculty is only listening to the inner Anahata sound, the skin faculty is indifferent to the atmospheric temperature, various changes, etc., the taste faculty is dormant, and the likes. Then the mind is fully dissolved in the wisdom of the intellect. The intellect now retraces itself in the pure and immaculate Atman. You can take the example of a tortoise. The tortoise retracts its own neck and head into its shell when it sees any external unwanted objects. The aspirant, through this practice, reaches a state where without the 'knowledge of the self', nothing else becomes prominent. By doing this, the aspirant keeps himself/herself in the ever-peaceful Atman or Jivatma.

ALERTING THE HUMAN BEINGS TO KNOW THE SELF!

Yama Raj is now speaking to alert the people to leave sleep, laziness, illusion, and ignorance. He says, "The human beings have the rare bodies by the grace of God. Now it forms a part of their duties to make all-out efforts to return to God's abode. They must leave all their vices and go to the wise, serve them and perform Satsang to know the process of making one's own welfare. By doing all these, the aspirants can understand the philosophies of God, the reason why we are bound in this world and the various spiritual processes following which we can elevate ourselves. The philosophies of God are very difficult to comprehend. The knowledge of the Brahman, the path to get Him are known only to the wise having full utilisation of their own conscience. In the hard and troublesome path of getting to God, the wise seem to be unwise and vice versa. The path to getting the Brahman and realising the self is so very difficult that we can compare this to walking on a sharp sword. When aspirants do their specified duties, there is every likelihood that they become unsuccessful and verily fall into deep holes. So, the support and the proper direction of the God-realised souls who possess the right experience are needed by the aspirants to comfortably cross the highly difficult and troublesome path leading to the knowledge of the Brahman."

THE REAL NATURE OF THE BRAHMAN:

Brahman is soundless, cannot be touched, has no shape, has no taste, and has no smell. He has no beginning and no end. He is constant. He is infinite without a beginning. He is greater than the greatest. He is Omnipotent, omniscient and Omnipresent. He is all-merciful and very impartial. He is the Truth. He is more powerful and more knowledgeable than the Atman or the Jivatma. He is the source of all sources. All works done by His creations are transitory. So, He is the cause of everything but does not have any contribution to the activities done by the Jivatma, which are not ordained by Him. This is precisely the reason why Brahman does not get engrossed in the worldly activities done by the Jivatma. He stares at the various activities of the Jivatma as a witness. Param Atma is subtler than the subtlest and greater than the greatest. When the human being knows about the Param Atma like this, he gets freed from the cycles of births and deaths.

SHRADDHA OR FAITH IS IMPORTANT:

The knowledge given to Nachiketa by Yama Raj can be received by the wise and by the persons having faith in God. It is the knowledge written in the Vedas and traditionally has the qualities of Sanatana (the oldest and having no beginning and no end). This knowledge is made for the welfare of the spiritual aspirants. The aspirants having due faith in the Brahman must know about Him from experienced Gurus. Such aspirants should also advise the disciples having deep faith in God. This way the proper spiritual path can be well trodden by the Gurus and the shishyas to duly know about the Brahman. Faith is very important to perform spiritual practices for Soul Elevation.

BENEFITS OF GIVING SPIRITUAL ADVICE TO A GROUP:

When a person with peace of mind carefully advises a group of aspirants about the philosophies of God or delivers the knowledge of God in various religious functions to a group of pure devotees, who are wise and erudite; then it becomes much more effective than speaking about the knowledge of God to one or 2 aspirants at a time. Basically, when we speak to one or a group of devotees at a time, we apply the same effort. So, deliberations to a group of people can bestow much better results than the former. In a group of, say, a hundred, maybe one or 2 can really understand and resort to spiritual Sadhana. For others, it may provide some encouraging information to think, meditate, etc., and decide later whether to go ahead with the process of Sadhana or just learn more about the philosophies of God and the processes, etc.

WHY THE CREATION OF THE INDRIYAS IS MADE BY GOD

Now a question arises as to the non-realisation of the Brahman. We have already stated that Brahman is present within us and is seated near our soul or our Atman. So, what is the reason that we are not able to see God by our internal intelligence? God has given us the external limbs to feel the various qualities. These are Sabda, Sparsa, Rupa, Rasa, and Gandha. All the limbs that are given the capabilities are known as Pancha Jnanendriyas. These Indriyas can listen, touch, see, taste, and smell using the external organs such as the ear, the skin, the eyes, the tongue, and the nose. God has given these Indriyas externally present in our body. The basic reason is that human beings will be able to use these Indriyas to get the various tattvas and enjoy them. Again, in the process of enjoyment, they will be able to know the bad effects of all these. After knowing the bad effects of the various qualities of the senses, human beings will now think inward and perform all the underlying processes to realise God using their intellect internally (known as Antar Drishti or the inward vision). These devotees study the Shrutis and the scriptures. Further, they make all efforts to follow the wise and listen to their advice to know the Brahman. Very rare wise after utilising these senses through their sense organs, make proper self-analysis, meditation, etc., and look inward. Finally, through their inner eyes, the respective devotees can be able to see or realise God.

The minds of the human beings get swayed away by the external tempting objects and their qualities. These human beings waste their valuable time in satisfying their own desires through various entertainments. These beings are fools. They know naught that all these sense pleasures bind them and because of these so-called pleasures, they move from womb to womb and must undergo myriads of cycles of births and deaths. By getting attached to the sense pleasures, freedom can never be achievable. On the contrary, the wise who are the true devotees of God behave very differently. They experience the sense pleasures and then conclude that all the sense pleasures are transitory in nature and they bind the human being. These sense pleasures never allow the human beings to attain the ultimate freedom. The main objective of getting the human body is to work towards God, to realise the Self and thereby know the Brahman eventually. Brahma Vidya is only obtained by very rare aspirants who turn all their resolve away from the sense enjoyment. Once the spiritual aspirants know the Brahman, they never come back from the realm of Satya Loka, which is the original abode of the Jivatma or the soul.

UNDERSTANDING THE EVER-CHANGING WORLD AND ITS VARIOUS OBJECTS:

By the grace of God, human beings can enjoy the sense objects like Sabda, Sparsa, Rupa, Rasa, and Gandha. In addition to this, the sexual union with the opposite sex and the experience of enjoyment from that activity. Now, all these experiences are done by the Jivatma, and by doing this, what remains? Nothing is permanent. Everything changes in each moment in this world. After realising the transitoriness of the worldly enjoyments, the Jivatma now understands the permanency or Nitya qualities of the Brahman. Brahman was present earlier and will also remain present in the future. This is the truth. God has given us the power of vision through our eyes. But without the medium, say the sunlight or the moonlight or any other light for that matter, can the eyes see? In a similar way, without the existence of air, can we listen to the various sounds? If we think like this, we can understand that without the support of Brahman, we have no existence. As we know that Brahman is the source of all sources and all the sources are His creation, so we need to shun everything and think of God only. Then only the path to freedom is possible.

GOD DISPOSES EVERYTHING IN THIS UNIVERSE:

By the grace of the Param Atman, the Jivatma can know various happenings repeatedly in the awakened and the dream states. This power of knowledge is only due to the support of the Param Atman. A part of His conscience is available to the Jivatma, using which it can know various happenings. Brahman is all-powerful and beyond all these powers. This is known to the meditative and the wise human beings. So, they do not feel distressed. Rather, they make all efforts to reach Him. These meditative human beings pray to the Lord before they go to bed. Because of their prayers, bad and horrible dreams never arise in their dreams. Basically, the calm and meditative persons do not dream. If by chance they see dreams, they never feel pained nor distressed. The meditative and calm persons who believe in the ubiquitousness of God during their awakened and dream states never feel bad or distressed in any of the happenings in the world. They have the only resolve that God disposes all. Human beings are to act on the path of spirituality as ordained by God.

WHAT HAPPENS WHEN KNOWLEDGE AWAKENS IN HUMAN BEINGS

Simply by knowing the Jivatma and the Param Atman, the human being has not achieved the whole or as desired by the Param Atman. The human being must realise that for every activity, the Param Atman is supreme. When the human being realises that 'Brahman is the bestower of all activities performed by the living beings'; 'He is the ruler of the past, the present and the future'; 'the saviour and the father of one and all'; 'is there as a witness', 'never gets attached to the various activities of the Jivatma'; 'free from pains and sufferings arising out of ignorance' and further the human being realises, 'Brahman is present in his/her heart of hearts and never deserts the subject or Jivatma'; then he verily realises the greatness of the Brahman and constantly finds Him within himself/herself. After having realised the Brahman in this manner; he/she never hates nor disparages/insults anyone. Such a wise person does not go to lower levels or to lower wombs after death. This is the supreme state of peace. Yama Raj says here to Nachiketa, "Look, these persons are in the state of peace and happiness. This is the Brahman, what you asked me to know about."

BRAHMAN IS PARAMESHWAR:

Brahman or the Param Atman or the Super Soul is the creator and the destroyer. During the demolition period, the worlds are filled with water. From the water, the various living beings are created by the express intent of the Brahman. He becomes obvious in the beginning. There was darkness everywhere during this period. This period is known as Pralay.

God now receives light through the ether or the sky. This sky is present everywhere. The different worlds are created thereafter, and then the living beings are created. Jivatma, due to its own folly, enters various living beings. Out of all living beings, human birth is supreme. The Jivatma sits in the body. Param Atman also remains very close to the Atman and observes the various activities of the Jivatma. The Super Soul or God is the Parameshwar and is the Lord of one and all. Yama Raj, thus describing, said to Nachiketa, "Dear boy, the Brahman about what you were asking me is this."

BHAGAVATI IS THE INSEPARABLE POWER OF God:

God has created His own creative power, namely Bhagavati. God and Bhagavati are inseparable. The same energy from God flows to Bhagavati. She has created all the demigods like all Indriyas (5 sensory nerves and 5 motor nerves that connect to the brain through various qualities such as Sabda, Sparsa, etc., and speech, the hands, the legs, the genital, and the solid excretory organ); the tanmaatras such as mind, intellect, memory, and ego, and finally the conscience duly obtained from the Brahman, the Pancha Bhutas (kshiti, Aap, etc.); the Pancha Vayu (Pran, Apan, Udan, Saman, and Vyana). So, she is the power of living (Jivani Shakti) of all living beings. Bhagavati is the mother of all demigods and the sole energy of all creations and demolitions. Since she is the only one, hence, her other name is "Aditi-one and only one." She is revealed through the creation of all living beings. Brahman is seated in the heart of hearts of the living beings along with Bhagavati. They are inseparable. "This is the Brahman what you asked me about, Oh my dear Nachiketa!"

The Indriyas have the tendencies to enjoy outward objects. Jivatma gets attracted by these outward attractions. This way the Jivatma becomes tethered. The wise tame or control the Indriyas by performing the processes of Pranayama (Extension of the breath-in and the breath-out cycle; in Sanskrit, Ayama means extension. So only, Pranayama is extending the Prana). Thus, by doing Pranayama as per the proper guidance of a guru, the intellect becomes as delicate as possible. Thereby, the Sadhakas can know the Brahman eventually. Our own internalities or the Antahkaran when work in its proper order, then realising or knowing the Brahman becomes easy for the true devotees or the Sadhakas. "Nachiketa, this is the Brahman what you wanted to know about," said Yama Raj.

BRAHMAN CAN BE KNOWN BY CONSTANT YOGA SADHANA:

"Nachiketa, you know that fire cannot be obtained without rubbing 2 wooden sticks (In the olden days, human beings were getting fire this way). In the same way, God, who is present in the core of our Antahkaran, will not become obvious without Yog Sadhana by the spiritual aspirants. Like a mother who is pregnant, makes the child in her womb grow by feeding (giving food and water) it regularly, similarly the wise and the erudite; the enquirer of the self; the yogi who is duly resolved in the path of truth; and who understands all the Vedas and the sacred fire thereof; who is responsible and takes utmost care to know or realise the Brahman; remembers God and works (performs Yog) for God incessantly. This is known as the worship of God, the Almighty. Oh! my dear Nachiketa, this is the Brahman about which you asked me," said Yama Raj.

ALL CREATIONS ARE UNDER THE ADMINISTRATIVE CONTROL OF THE BRAHMAN:

Sun and all other planets and stars are created by God. During the Pralay period, all the planets along with the Sun also get demolished. Owing to the magnanimity of the Brahman, the Sun rises and sets by maintaining its proper time. Exactly each creation of God abides by the rules made by God. This Brahman, who is Omni Potent, Omnipresent, and omniscient and who resides in each living being, thus becomes the source of all. No one has the capabilities to transgress or disobey the rules made by the Brahman. Brahman has a conscience better than everything, and this is precisely the reason we say, "Man proposes and God disposes. This is the truth, and each of us should understand this. Another aspect of Brahman is that, though He knows everyone and controls everyone, no one knows about His limits. He is all-powerful Param Purush. Dear Nachiketa, this is the Brahman, what you asked me to know," said Yama Raj.

BRAHMAN IS CONSTANT/UNCHANGEABLE/ONE AND WITHOUT A SECOND:

This Brahman or the Param Atman or God or Param Purush is one. He has no name and no form. He is not to be thought or construed as different. This Atman moves from womb to womb and takes birth in various bodies from birth to birth. This cycle is unending until the Atman gets a human body by the grace of the Lord and from there on performs Sadhana for Soul Elevation to enter the realm of God, which is known as Satya Loka. Now when the Atman takes birth in different bodies, its characteristics change. But the characteristics of the Param Atman never change. The Param Atman is always constant, unchanging, and one without a second. He exists in this world and exists in all other worlds of this universe. Atman has no friend and has no enemies. He does not undergo birth and rebirth like Atman. He is the knower of everything. He has no father nor a mother. He has no guru, neither does he have a disciple (Shishya). Being the maintainer of one and all, and having His presence everywhere, He is seen differently by the ignorant. This is the reason why the Atman takes birth in different bodies. This Atman when it takes birth in a different world gets the name of the Brahman differently. But the same Param Atman is present everywhere. Now, the question is, how can the Atman in a human body become free from cycles of births and deaths. First, the Sadhak should have a firm belief that the Param Atman is one and without a second. He is very merciful. He wants the Atman to work towards getting itself free from the clutches of repeated birth. This Brahman is pure and ever-blissful.

ONE AND ONLY ONE WAY TO GET BRAHMAN:

There are not many ways to get to God or Brahman. To reach God, one should clearly and with a pure mind follow the path depicted and duly ordained in the Vedas; resort to deep meditation. This is the only way to understand the philosophies of God and truly realise Him. By performing this Sadhana, the aspirant will be able to understand that Brahman is all-pervasive and that everything we behold in this universe is Brahman. There is no other way to purify one's own mind. A person who speaks of various methods to reach God, has different views, names, and forms of God, and this is not the truth. These people can never be freed and will indeed fall into the continuous cycles of birth and death.

THE SEAT OF BRAHMAN IS THE HEART OF ALL BEINGS:

We all agree that God was there, is there, and will be there. It means God has no beginning and has no end. Though He is all-pervasive, yet God remains in the heart of each being. As an example, God remains in the minute heart of an ant, and God also remains in the large heart of an elephant. It is said that the size of a human heart can be compared with that of a thumb (Angustha). God verily remains in our heart. God is neither subtle nor gross; He is neither small nor big. What does this mean? If air, which is created by God, is present everywhere, then only God is also present everywhere. He is so small when residing in the heart of the smallest being and is so large when seated in the heart of the largest being. This is the beauty of God. As we see our face in a mirror, in the same manner, the yogi visualises God in the heart when he meditates with a pure mind. Unless our mind is pure and still, we cannot see God. Even if we try to see inside our heart, the image of God will seem blurred. You can take the example of the reflection of the full Moon in still water during autumn. If the water has waves, then the Moon's image will be blurred. So, a mind that is not calm cannot see the pure image of God in the heart. When the spiritual aspirant sees the existence of God in the heart, his doubts get cleared. By this, he realises the basic characteristics (Omnipresence, Omni-science, and Omni-potence) of God. After this realisation, before any wrongdoing by him, he fears. In the same way, for all good doings, he gets happiness and cheerfulness from inside. Again, after knowing the presence of God in every being, the aspirant does neither hate nor insult anyone. He remains in a cheerful mind always. He thinks everyone is equal because all are the creations of the one Brahman.

"Oh, my dear Nachiketa! This is the Brahman about which you are interested to know," said Yama Raj.

GOD IS PEACEFUL, HAS JYOTI, AND IS SANATANA:

"We have seen the creations of the suns, the stars, and the fires by God. They are hot. But God, having seated in the Angustha-shaped heart of every individual, is quite bright, but there is no heat in Him. He is calm and quiet. His brilliance is pure, divine, clean, and peaceful. The light emitted by the Brahman has a brilliancy better than all brilliant lights that we have come across. All the natural lights have smoke. But God's own brilliant light (Jyoti) is not polluted by smoke. All the lights created by God increase and decrease over time. These natural lights also get extinguished eventually. But the Jyoti of God is constant, and it does not end. It is never polluted by any external agencies also. God is Sanatana, which means He has no beginning and no end. He is not changeable. This Brahman never changes, never dies, and was neither created by anyone. So, my dear Nachiketa! This is the Brahman about what you are interested to know," said Yama Raj.

GOD IS WORSHIPPED DIFFERENTLY BY LIVING BEINGS: THEY ARE BOUND:

"As the same water falls from the clouds on the mountains and flows across topsy-turvy surfaces, its colour and characteristics get changed due to contamination. But the water when it comes to the ground by the rain of the clouds has the same characteristics all through. In the same manner, various types of beings starting from insects, birds, animals, demons, demigods, and human beings, etc., are created by the same Brahman. But due to their ignorance, they worship the Brahman in various names and forms. But the God of the demons, and the God of the demigods or the God of the human beings are no different from each other. God or Brahman or the creator is one and the same for all. This is precisely the reason (like the various waters from the same cloud), these demigods, demons, and human beings must take birth in various bodies through the respective wombs. They have no respite from the shackles of the cycles of birth and death."

"But if the pure water from the clouds falls on pure water due to rain, then at the same moment the water becomes pure undoubtedly. No pollution, no change of external characteristics, etc. are possible. And this pure water also never goes anywhere. So, my dear Nachiketa! The persons who know about this properly, those meditative great beings, become pure and get the Brahman eventually," said Yama Raj.

Now the discussion between Yama Raj and Nachiketa has given us an insight into the Brahman and provided inspiration to all spiritual aspirants to work towards elevating one's own soul.

THE ELEVEN DOORS, VARNASHRAMA, AND REPAYING THE 3 DEBTS:

Our body has 11 doors (ekadash dwar). These are Brahmarandhra (the small hole on the top of our head. Through this hole, life enters and exits), 2 eyes, 2 ears, 2 noses, mouth, navel, upastha (sex organ), paayu (anus). Our body is like a city, and the monarch of this city is the Brahman. We have already discussed the various characteristics of this monarch. Now, the human being must complete its life run across the 4 Varnashramas (Brahmacharya, grihastha, vanaprastha, and sannyasa) in all piousness and as per the laws of nature with due obligation to God. Again, during this lifetime, the human being must repay the 3 debts before leaving this world. The 3 loans are:

1. Pitri Rin (Debt that we owe to our parents, because they have given us birth and maintained us until we are able to manage ourselves independently)

2. Rishi Rin (Debt that we owe to the various sages, because they have written the scriptures to give us knowledge)

3. Deva Rin (Debt owing to the demigods because we are living because they provide us air, water, fire, atmosphere, land, and the likes such as ether).

After repaying these 3 debts, human beings should perform sadhanas to elevate their souls to realise the Brahman. Human beings should shun the false knowledge that binds them and follow the principles of God to elevate themselves. Human beings must resort to self-analysis through deep meditation to be freed. These human beings, due to their spiritual Sadhana, finally visualise the Brahman by His mercy. This knowledge of Brahman was asked for by Nachiketa to Yama Raj.

GOD EXISTS EVERYWHERE:

This Brahman is beyond all the characteristics of nature. Because He is the creator of all these. He is verily the Purodha (owner who institutes) or the Hota (in Sanskrit) of all the yajnas. He is seated in the Satya Lok and is Purushottama. He moves in the ethereal spheres and is also known as Vasu. He is present in the space of the hearts of all living beings. He is also seated in all aquatic animals like the fish, the turtles, and the seahorses, etc. He is also present in the forests, in the deserts, on the mountains, and everywhere that one can think of and cannot think of. He is established in all living beings and is the master of everyone. He is established as the saints, the demigods, and the forefathers who are superior to all human beings. He is established in the Akasa and in the truth. He is revealed in medicinal plants, the rivers, the lakes, the oceans, etc. He is present in foods, in the havan, and in the results obtained from the yajnas that are performed by the human beings having no desires. The human beings who are pure at heart, whose works are in line with achieving the ultimate truth, who remember the powers, and the magnificence of God at all times are deserved to meet the Brahman will not have rebirth in this world.

GOD CONTROLS OUR BODY:

By the mercy of God, we breathe and thereby maintain our lives. The Pran Vayu flows in our body in the upper zone, i.e. from the naval to the nose, to the head, to the brain, etc. The Apan Vayu flows downward, i.e. from the naval to the genital organ and to the anus, etc. Pran and Apan Vayu are provided by God. God is seated in our hearts like Vaman (Vaman means a dwarf human being who came to the world as the incarnation of God to diminish the false ego of the demon king namely Mahavali). So, we should construe Vaman (another name of God) as very minute, who is seated in our heart. All the Indriyas, the mind, the intellect, the memory cells, and all our external and internal organs are performing their duties carefully owing to the spiritual directives and inspiration of God.

WHAT HAPPENS WHEN A BODY DIES

We have known that the Soul and Super Soul have neither a beginning nor an end. But the body dies. After the death of a body, the soul moves out of the body. At that time, the soul takes the Antahkaran (mind, intellect, memory, and ego) along with the Indriyas in subtle forms. The dead body has nothing. But what remains in this dead body is the Brahman. Yama Raj explains thus about Brahman to Nachiketa. Here the most merciful quality of the Brahman is that He is present in all beings, either living or dead.

We have already understood that our soul is the subtlest of all other devas such as the Indriyas, the mind, the intellect, etc. So, who is the source of the Vayu (Pran and Apan)? The simple answer is, 'the soul.' So, our soul being the source, if present in the body, even the Pran and the Apan Vayu do not flow, yet the body is alive because of the existence of the soul in it. When a saint takes Samadhi (a state when he neither breathes in nor breathes out), people mistakenly think that the body is dead. But this is not correct. The soul is in the body, and hence the saint is alive. The Pran and Apan take shelter in the soul. Then how can the body die! So, the knowledge that the body is dead during the Samadhi state is 'false knowledge.' From this, we clearly understand that the superior most and the source of our body is the soul. This soul is also known as Jivatma.

Yama Raj further states to Nachiketa what happens to the Jivatma after it leaves the body along with the Antahkaran and the Indriyas! What happens to the Jivatma after the death of the body? Where does it go and where does it stay? In addition, the real nature of the all-pervasive, all-powerful, all-knowledgeable Super Soul will also be explained by me. Please listen to me carefully.

Yama Raj said, "The soul or Jivatma enters the mother's womb through the father's semen to get a body based on certain factors: such as the knowledge gained from the scriptures, from Sadguru (A Brahman realised person is known as a Sadguru), the last desire of the person based on his/her experience from the environment. Since in the past birth, the person did not make any efforts for God realisation, the types of mother's womb depend on his/her good or bad work during the lifetime. These wombs are categorised as good, medium, and inferior (Uttam, Madhyam and Nikrusta respectively). Thus, having undergone a rebirth through the respective womb, the new body is bound to get into the worldly pains and sorrows. The lives whose good and bad work are equal, he/she gets a human body. The lives who had more bad work than good work, he/she enters the womb of an animal or the womb of that of a bird etc. The lives that performed very high bad work enter the various bodies which are static in nature, such as trees, creepers, grass or even the soul enters the womb of a stone. From this statement of Yama Raj, God exists in all entities living or non-living."

After describing the movement of the Jivatma to a new body through its womb, Yama Raj is now explaining the Swaroop of Param Atman. He said, "The Super Soul is always there, i.e. from creation to demolition (Srusti to Pralay) and again during creation. However, during Pralay, each Jivatma loses its knowledge. Brahman, being omniscient, never loses His memory or knowledge. Also, His knowledge does not vary at any point in time. This is why we know Him as Param Brahman. All the Lokas starting from Bhuh are under His active control. No one can supersede Him. All are subordinate to Him. Oh, dear Nachiketa! This is the Brahman about which you were interested to know."

COMPARING FIRE AND ITS NATURE WITH THAT OF THE BRAHMAN:

For an easy understanding, Yama Raj took the example of fire. He said, "Fire is one. It does not have a size or a shape. Fire is not attached to anything. The volume and extent of fire are based on the size and the shape of the entity. When there is fire in the forest, it is vast. But when fire burns firewood, it takes a smaller shape than it had while burning a portion of a forest. Exactly, God takes shape accordingly and is not attached to anyone. When fire burns a forest, it does not leave any entity. Whosoever comes in its purview, it burns and never gets attached to anyone. This is also the characteristic of Brahman. His extent could be small or large based on the body, and He remains unattached and impartial irrespective. Apart from the Swaroop and the greatness of Brahman, there are many celestial qualities present in Brahman. One can think that a small portion of Brahman is present in all entities and provides energy to one and all." Here we also know that Brahman has created fire.

COMPARING AIR AND ITS SWAROOP WITH THAT OF THE BRAHMAN:

Yama Raj took another example to explain about the Brahman. Here he took the example of air (Vayu). All of us know that we cannot live without air. Air blows and we feel it. But we are not able to see air. It is very subtle in nature. In a similar manner, Brahman is the source of every entity in the universe. Brahman does not reveal itself to anyone. As it is present by the side, inside, outside, near, and far from an entity, in the same manner, Brahman is present here and there, inside, and outside, near, and far, etc. Brahman is the source of all entities of the universe. This air is infinite, having different volumes based on the extent of the entity, has different energy levels based on the situations, etc. Brahman accommodates everything as it is Omnipotent and provides energy to one and all. Brahman has no beginning and no end. So, Brahman is infinite. Here we also know that air is created by Brahman. Only for easy understanding, this example is given here.

EXAMPLES OF THE SUN AND MOON ARE GIVEN HERE:

We know that all entities of this universe are created by God. But for easy understanding about the brilliance and non-attachment, Yama Raj took the examples of the Sun and Moon. The Sun gives light and heat energy to everyone. The Moon, also taking light from the Sun, gives light to the Earth. We say that our right eye is the Sun and the left eye is the Moon. Our eyes, by the brilliance of both the Sun and the Moon, are lighted. Exactly in the same manner, Brahman has its own light and by His own brilliancy, provides intellect and conscience to the various entities starting from human beings. Though the Sun and Moon provide light to everyone without any discrimination, they are not attached. By the grace of Brahman, we can get energies for our intellect, mind, and the Indriyas. Brahman being present in everyone's heart knows everything about us. So, He is termed as 'Antaryami'. Getting power from God, the various

Indriyas and our Antahkaran get inspired to perform both good and bad work and are bound to get both pain and pleasure, which are temporary. However, Brahman is unattached and remains very indifferent from all these performances. In gist, we can say that Brahman remains unattached by the actions of the Jivatma and does not make friends with anyone.

WHICH ASPIRANT GETS HAPPINESS BEING IN THE WORLD

All the aspirants work to get God. But there are levels. When the aspirant fully understands that God is all-powerful and everyone is below His powers, when he/she understands that 'Man proposes and God disposes', when he/she understands that God is everywhere and that's why he/she sees everyone as one and the same, when he/she neither humiliates nor hates anyone because the same Param Atman is seated near the Jivatma of everyone, when he/she understands that God is very merciful, impartial and non-attached. Such a person does all work surrendering the results to God, such a spiritual aspirant lives happily even in this world. However, all others do not get such happiness.

When Satya, Sanatan, Param Purush is seated in all beings without any difference, how can an aspirant see the difference? If God has stated that each and everyone should do unattached work, how can anyone do work with a desire for fruit? If the Jivatma is a part of the Param Atma, then how can a spiritual practitioner find differences in Jivatma and Param Atma? It is understood that this difference is seen only by an ignorant. The pure devotees of the Lord think of God always: in all works, in the awakened and in the dream states (details of the various states are discussed after this), everywhere and in all moments through meditation; then only such a devotee or a spiritual aspirant can live in peace and happiness in this world. All others cannot find such happiness and peace while living in this world. In summary, one can state that a devotee who becomes Godward and sees God in proper meditation lives happily in this world.

THE WHOLE UNIVERSE IS ILLUMINATED BY GOD (BRAHMAN):

After listening to the characteristics and the Swaroop of Brahman from Yama Raj, his disciple Nachiketa was thinking all about Purushottama. He was thinking, when Brahman is the creator of everything in this universe, how to see Him. How can I have the direct knowledge of God? God is all-powerful, and His brilliancy is much brighter than that of the sun, the stars, the lightning, and any entity having brilliancy. God gives shining to everyone. He is the light of the lights, He is the Vayu of Vayu, He is the fire of fire, and He is the rain of rain. No one is beyond Him. Only the yogis can see Him through pure and deep meditation. And not only that, but the Spiritual aspirant also who can see God by deep meditation must have been chosen by the Brahman Himself! Hence, unless a spiritual aspirant who does Purushartha or Spiritual Practices (Spiritual Sadhana) for Soul Elevation must be a pure devotee of God.

OUR BODY IS COMPARED TO AN INVERTED PEEPAL TREE:

"The human body is compared with an inverted peepal tree (Aswath Briksh in Sanskrit). The head is construed as the root of the tree, and the branches are projected towards the ground. This philosophy is treated as pure. This tree is dependent on the mercy of God who is Sanatan, i.e. having no beginning and no end."

"Now we must understand the Pinda-Brahmanda philosophy. Here the whole universe is also treated as an inverted peepal tree. On the root is the Brahman. The demigods, human beings, animals, and birds have tilted downward, and they are the branches of this large tree. This divine tree is Sanatan or having no beginning nor an end. God, who is the subtlest of all, is seated at the top or at the root and is controlling all beings of the whole universe. This is the concept. All Vedas, all Yagnas, all good and bad work, and their results thereof are seated in the various leaves of this peepal tree."

"This inverted tree is present from infinity and is visible and invisible at different periods of time. This peepal tree exists as per the wish of God. And because of this, the divine tree has no beginning nor an end. The safety and maintenance of this divine tree are vested in the Brahman. No one is beyond the ever-existing Brahman. Know about this Brahman, dear Nachiketa," said Yama Raj during the discussion.

This world is created by the Lord. So, whatever we hear, whatever we touch, whatever we see, whatever we taste, and whatever we smell, all are controlled by God. We do not have an iota of ideas about all these. God is the sound of the sound, touch of the touch, vision of the vision, taste of the taste, and smell of the smell. The yogi who knows about this is pure and will never say that he knows the Brahman. Unless our ego is burnt asunder, we cannot elevate our own souls and realise Him. If we see that the Sun, the Moon, the stars, and all the celestial entities are doing their duties in line with proper disciplines, it is only due to God. The soul who has forgotten its duties and enjoyed through its Indriyas in the body, after getting painful experiences once and again in different birth and death cycles, begins to tread its path to reach God; so that eventually the ever-wandering Jivatma reaches Satyaloka and will never return to the different worlds that are transient and the sources of pains and sufferings. These pure souls are the yogis or the Sadhakas or the spiritual aspirants as we call them.

BRAHMAN: THE RULER AND CONTROLLER OF EVERYONE:

By this time, we have understood that Brahman is one and only one. He is impartial and sentient. He is the root of all creations. Each creation of the Brahman is controlled by Him, and He administers all the planets, the stars, the nebulas, the comets, and what not. The Sun fears Him. Out of fear, the Sun gives hotness and moves in the sky as per scheduled times; the fire is giving heat and burning various entities or objects, including the living and the non-living. The air or Vayu flows obeying the orders of the Brahman. Due to the flow of air, the living beings are surviving. Death takes out life from the living beings on time by His orders. So the creations, maintenance, and demotion cycle are duly controlled by the Brahman. All these celestial and divine entities perform their duties as ordained by the Brahman or by God. Speaking in one sentence, we can say that God is the controller, the administrator of each and everything in the universe. All worlds and all celestial entities abide by the Brahman with due meticulousness.

KNOWLEDGE OF THE BRAHMAN BEFORE DEATH IS NECESSARY TO BE FREE:

The living human beings, if they know before their death that Brahman is the ruler, the controller, the Supreme who is to be known, then only they will find out ways and means to reach God. They will verily go to a

God-realised soul and get well-trained by them in the process or the paths to reach God. So, after their death, they completely elevate their souls by performing Spiritual Sadhana and never repent that during their life they could not find time to resort to the processes of Soul Elevation. These yogis finally realise God and get fully mingled with God and never return to take repeated births and deaths in this transitory world.

BHUH LOKA IS SUITABLE TO KNOW THE BRAHMAN AND GET HIM:

All the human beings are in the Bhuh Loka. The other Lokas are Bhuvah, Swah, Mahah, Janah, Tapa and Satya Loka. Our forefathers usually stay in the Bhuvah Loka or in the Swah Loka. The angels stay in the Swah Loka. Some angels stay in the Mahah or Janah Loka who are still purer and have elevated their souls to stay in these levels. The highly elevated saints stay in the Tapa Loka. Based on the elevation levels, the various noble souls stay in different Lokas or levels. Satya Loka is the ultimate Loka where the Brahman resides along with the various freed souls. A human being, if desiring to stay in the Pitri Loka (Bhuvah or Swah Loka), then the Brahman is not clear to him/her. Brahman is like a bright Sun, having much more brightness than the Sun. As in muddy water the Sun's reflections look blurred, in the same way, in the Pitri Loka, Brahman is very unclear. Similarly, in the layers where the angels reside, the Brahman can be seen, who is a little clearer than in the Pitri Lokas. As the levels get elevated, the clarity of the Brahman increases till the yogi ascends to the level of Satya Loka where he/she resides with the Brahman or God. Hence after knowing about all the levels or the Lokas, the Yogi or the Sadhaka should perform Sadhana to reach God in the human birth (in Bhuh Loka) only, failing which he/she is subject to fall into the repetitive cycles of births and deaths.

FEELING THE SELF AND NOT THE BODY MAKES ONE FREE FROM SORROWS:

There is a word in Sanskrit known as 'Dehabhimana' or the ego of one's own body. Until we understand and identify ourselves as this body, we are bound. Though we discussed that Jivatma enjoys through the various Indriyas and therefore gets involved in repeated birth and death cycles, it turns away from these sense pleasures eventually by the grace of God through repeated human births after doing mostly good works in life and very few bad works. The Jivatma understands that though Param Atman is sitting very near, still He is not involved in the body, its Antahkarans, and the Indriyas. When the wise experiences that the awakened state and the dream states are changeable and never have any permanency and understands in the deep sleep or slumber state, all the feelings get absorbed and nothing is available; and then the thought of God comes to the mind of the Sadhaka, and he/she starts thinking of getting out of the shackles of the worldly tethers. All these experiences make the wise realise that he/she is not this body. He is the Atman or the self and is a part of the very merciful, all-powerful, and all-knowledgeable Param Atman. These feelings verily make the spiritual aspirant decide to go back to his/her real abode, and that is the abode of God from where he/she has come out by a mere desire.

VIVEKA (CONSCIENCE) SPROUTS IN THE MINDS OF THE WISE:

At this point in time, the spiritual aspirant understands that God is the creator, the maintainer, and He is the annihilator. This way the cycles are maintained in the universe. The Jivatma has no respite in the realm of darkness, and that is the world. Once this tattva of God is clearly understood, which is known as Viveka (conscience: the feeling of oneness of God, who is the truth and all others are illusion), then the person truly becomes a spiritual aspirant to become one with God. This way he/she looks for a guru or a Spiritual Guide who is established in the Brahman to show the aspirant the proper path to God.

THE SADHAK HAS VAIRAGYA (DISPASSION) THEREAFTER:

As soon as the Viveka sprouts in the minds of the wise, the next quality that enters is vairagya or dispassion. In this state, the wise clearly understand that all the activities projected towards the satisfaction of the Indriyas are illusory in nature that give pains and sorrows. In this state, the wise understand that Stambha to Brahma, all are temporary in nature. This body is transitory. Only Brahman is the truth. Lord Brahma is also not permanent. This is the quality of vairagya or dispassion.

THE SADHAKA MAKES SENSE CONTROL OR SAMA:

Sama is regarded as one of the 6 wealths (Sat-Sampatti). This means controlling one's own mind by identifying the bad effects of pleasure arising out of Indriyas. All sense pleasures are temporary in nature and cause pain. Once a spiritual aspirant understands this, he/she will not be swayed away by the attraction of our various senses. Rather, the aspirant will concentrate on the real objectives of getting to God.

THE SADHAKA MAKES MIND CONTROL OR DAMA:

All the objects of sense pleasures are enjoyed when the respective Indriya such as the ear, skin, eye, tongue, or/and the nose is/are involved in it. Every Indriya has an orb in our brain. The Sadhaka, by the proper guidance of a guru, retracts the Indriyas to their respective orbs and because of this, the Sadhaka's mind gets duly controlled. Please remember, controlling the mind is very difficult; it is something like keeping a very small amount of mercury on the tip of a needle. So, this great wealth once acquired by a Sadhaka, by the grace of a guru and by dint of constant practice, leads to perfect mind control in ours.

SADHAKA HAS UPARATI AS AN ESSENTIAL QUALITY:

Our mind is very unstable. It has the characteristics to go outside and get disturbed often. We have various openings (openings of the 2 ears, the 2 eyes, the 2 noses, the various pores of our skin and the likes) in our body. This is precisely the reason why the mind gets distracted owing to the external disturbances through the various openings in our body. The distraction of our mind is known as Mano-Vritti. You can take an example of a tub where water is reserved. If there exists a small hole in the tub, then the water gets leaked. In a similar manner, our mind gets away and cannot concentrate as desired for a long period of time. Yogi or the Sadhaka needs their minds to be steady and not get swayed away by the external disturbances or happenings. It is something like retracing one's own mind towards its seat in the brain. In that state, if the eyes are seeing, still it is not seeing because the mind is not accompanied by the vision. Similarly, in that state, the ear is hearing, but it is not hearing because the mind is not there. So, who is subtler than the Indriyas? It is the mind. You must have seen a turtle. When it sees some external objects or unknown living beings, it immediately retracts its head inside its own shell. This is needed for the mind. All best Uparatis are when the mind is not attached to external disturbances.

TITIKSHA (ENDURANCE) IS ANOTHER QUALITY OF THE SADHAKA:

A yogi should not be perturbed by the various climatic changes. You must have felt that we get highly disturbed when there are changes in the atmospheric temperatures. Again, there are various situations, such as happiness or sorrowfulness, etc. The yogi is supposed to be steadfast in all circumstances. If the yogi is experiencing physical pain due to ill health, still he/she should not get perturbed. The yogi should have the qualities of perseverance and tolerance. The yogi is supposed to tolerate the situations whatsoever, without resorting to any treatment to quell the effects of heat, cold, and the like. We are taught in the scriptures to treat respect and humiliation as one and the same. This way, the yogi should have the quality of Titiksha or endurance.

SHRADDHA (UNWAVERING FAITH) IS ONE OF THE QUALITIES:

What the scriptures proclaim is the truth. What the guru tells us or advises us to perform is the truth. This should be well understood by the yogi and believed with unwavering faith. Then only can we say that the Sadhaka has Shraddha. Please remember, a yogi without Shraddha can never climb to the higher rung of Soul Elevation. A doubting self without clarity of thought processes always makes a yogi unsuccessful in achieving the goal.

We have studied that the scriptures say, "TATTWAMASI: THAT THOU ART." We have to believe in this philosophy, and only then can we practice this statement to progress on the path of freedom.

SAMADHANA (CONCENTRATION OF THE MIND IN THE PURE BRAHMAN):

What is pure Brahman! When there are no qualities, when there is no shape or size, when it is not attached to anything yet is the master of all, is the pure Brahman.

Next consideration is the mind. Our mind is the creator and the destroyer of all of us. 'Sankalp-Vilalpatmak Manah.' It means our mind decides to do and does not decide to do. When our mind decides to do something positive, then only we get good results and when it decides to do something unwanted, we get bad results. Now here is a different quality for the Sadhaka that we are discussing to aid to Soul Elevation. The mind has variability of thought processes. Now let us make an exercise, so that the mind is placed on pure Brahman. The mind is not allowed by the yogi to move here and there. It should only concentrate on the pure Brahman. This is a very important quality the yogi should have, so that all vibrations of the mind are quelled. Again, it is needed that this state is to be maintained always then only the yogi can be able to visualise the self and thus can also meet the Brahman. All yogis should practise their best to have SAMADHAN.

We have already discussed the 6 qualities (Sat-Sampatti) for a yogi. Now let us discuss another important quality that a yogi should have! This is known as Mumukshutva.

MUMUKSHUTVA:

Yearning for liberation is termed in Sanskrit as Mumukshutva. Unless the spiritual aspirant realises that he/she is not free, this interest will not arise with the yogi or the aspirant.

We have already stated that ego binds everyone. In addition to this, we cannot identify when ego attacks us. It has a very thin line (between ego and being egoless). By speaking or doing something, ego in us sprouts. And thereby we are bound. Similarly, the other vices in us are attachment, anger, greed, indulgence in luxury, jealousy, etc. If we think with due attention, we can understand that due to these vices in us, we are bound. Then what is the solution? It is 'knowing the self.' Knowing one's own self is the first step to elevate our own souls.

If we summarise, we have seen that a successful spiritual aspirant should have Viveka or conscience; vairagya or dispassion; Sat-Sampatti (the 6 wealths: Sama, Dama, Uparati, Titiksha, Shraddha, and Samadhan); and finally Mumukshutva (yearning for liberation) to elevate his/her soul. Apart from this, we could also understand from the discussion between Yama Raj and Nachiketa that the blessings of the Lord should also be there to achieve the goal.

Again, we should keep it well in our minds that yearning for liberation should be very acute, then only there is a possibility to proceed up and up. This is the basic secret of attaining salvation.

BRAHMAN IS THE OWNER:

Jivatma is the owner of our body, and the owner of Jivatma is the Brahman. All Indriyas are at the lowest ebb. Still, subtle to them is our mind. The Jivatma enjoys this world based on its mind's action. The moment Jivatma understands that it is not doing the right thing as a human being, from that moment, the Jivatma turns its actions towards satisfying the basic directives of the Brahman. This is Spiritual Elevation of the Soul or the Jivatma. Jivatma has clearly understood that this body is not its real abode. He has to seek the abode of Param Atman, what we call as Satya Loka.

Brahman sitting near the Jivatma always becomes a silent observer. By its own kindness, the Jivatma has got the rare human body. All human beings should realise that they have got the rare human body and without wasting further time, they should perform Purushartha to meet God and stay there permanently. Thus, they will become free from the repeated cycles of birth and death. If by any chance they miss this opportunity, they are not sure whether in the next birth they will get a human birth or not. To get a human birth once more, human beings are required to perform right actions during their own lifetime. This is the secret.

HOW THE JIVATMA SEES THE DIVINE SWAROOP OF PARAM ATMAN

This is a very interesting matter. Jivatma being very near to the Param Atman is not able to know His Swaroop. Human beings cannot see Param Atman with their eyes. To see Him, they must undergo lots of penances and do good work besides resorting to deep meditation on pure Brahman as we discussed earlier. So, our inner eye can see the Swaroop of Brahman if He blesses us in addition to our Purushartha. Like a bird has 2 wings, in a similar manner, to reach God, we should have 2 things. One is the performance of Spiritual Sadhana and the other is the blessings of God. These 2 together can lead us to meet God. This is as per the Vedas.

The so-called Indriyas (The Pancha Jnanendriyas: ear, skin, etc., and the Pancha Karmendriyas: tongue, hands, etc.) cannot see God. Our Antahkarans (such as our mind, intellect, memory, and ego) cannot see God. Brahman is beyond the limits of all these. But the person who has an ardent desire of seeing God can get Him for sure. If this is not agreed to by the persons, then how can God be available to them! Faith is one of the ways to get God. A strong faith leads us to light. As we discussed earlier, the Sadhaka must control the Indriyas, the mind, and the Antahkarans to know and get God. Be Godward, my dear friend. This is the inspiration stated in all the scriptures (scriptures are the shastras that discuss the self, the non-self, the Brahman, the processes to attain the Almighty).

CONVICTION THAT GOD IS THERE:

The Sadhakas must possess strong and unwavering conviction that God is there and is present in the heart of the hearts of one and all. Furthermore, they should have a clear conviction that by doing the Purushartha, God will be available for sure. Those people who have very strong faith in God can get God for sure without fail or without an iota of doubt. For all the Sadhakas who have Shraddha and the right conviction, God appears before them through their meditative eyes.

The human being is fraught with all sorts of desires: of the past, the present, and the future. He/she is not fully away from these desires. Even a person desires to get a human body after he enters the next birth and death cycle. This is why his/her actions are oriented accordingly to getting various desired results. But this is the binding force, i.e. 'The desire!' The moment the human beings think that 'everything is disposed of by God and he/she is a mere player in the world,' and then only he/she will start performing in line with the wishes of God and not act as per his/her own wishes. All wishes of human beings then become secondary or out of place. This is the state where the human beings strongly seek after getting God in this human birth. We say in other words, a strong yearning for liberation has sprouted in the life of the respective human being.

All human beings are bound by the knots of ignorance. These knots are to be cut asunder. Only then does the possibility of meeting God in our heart of hearts become bright and eventually possible. The razor is knowledge here. The knots of ignorance are to be cut by the razor of wisdom or knowledge. This is written in the Upanishads to reach God. So, the transition is from the realm of ignorance to the realm of wisdom, the realm of light, the realm of permanent freedom. Only by being in this human body, the Sadhaka meets God and becomes deathless by not being born again. This advice is known as 'Sanatan Upadesha' as written in the Vedas.

In our heart, there are 101 chief astral nerves. Out of them, the most important astral nerve is known as Susumna. This Susumna nerve traverses from our heart to the brain. The successful spiritual aspirant goes to the permanent, peaceful, and deathless abode of God through Susumna while leaving their body. All others leave their body through the nerves other than Susumna. Thereby they fall into the repeated cycles of birth and death.

All the spiritual aspirants understand the difference between the Jivatma and the Param Atman. They understand the superiority of Param Atman over Jivatma. They clearly visualise the leadership of the Param Atman. But the ignorant never want to seek God. They do not believe in the existence of God and are bound in the sorrowful and painful world.

We have 3 states (Avastha): Jagrat (the state of awakening), Swapna (dream state), and Sushupti (state of slumber). The 3 states are discussed in detail later.

Our Spirit, Atma, or our soul resides in our heart during the state of slumber. It stays in our throat during the dream state and resides in our pupils during the awakened state. This soul is covered by 5 sheaths or Koshas. These 5 sheaths are known as Annamaya or the food-only sheath; Pranamaya Kosha or the air-only sheath; Manomaya Kosha or the mind-only sheath; Vijnanamaya Kosha or the intellect-only sheath; and Anandmaya Kosha or the Blissful sheath. All these sheaths construct our body.

STHULA SHARIRA OR THE GROSS BODY:

Out of these sheaths, Annamaya Kosha is our body hardware such as the bones, marrow, blood, skin, fat, flesh, various cells, tissues, the various systems like the digestive, the respiratory, the circulatory, the urinogenital systems etc. The limbs are also made by the Annamaya Kosha. These limbs are: the hands, the legs, our chest, arms, our head and our back etc. This body is the basis of Avidya or ignorance or delusion. We identify ourselves with our body because of Avidya or ignorance. We have no knowledge of our own soul.

As we eat various foods, different limbs get formed and grow eventually. Some foods are responsible for the growth of our middle parts like bone marrow. If we eat ghee or clarified butter, our bone marrow gets more vitality and its growth becomes better. We get energy from foods like carbohydrates. Proteins become the source of growth for our body parts because they maintain our tissues, provide structure, and maintain proper pH, etc.

Because of our body, which is otherwise known as the Sthula Sharira, the words like 'I,' 'my' come up in our mind. We start saying, 'my pen', 'I discussed', 'I swam' etc. This extreme attachment to our body due to delusion, we forget that the soul is everything and not this. Other than identifying ourselves as our body, we need to identify as the soul. We need to say, 'I am Atman.' 'Atman and Param Atman are one and the same.' Therefore, we are in ignorance.

We discussed the Sthula Sharira and its composition. Now let us discuss the Pancha Bhutas or the 5 basic elements.

PANCHA BHUTAS:

The Pancha Bhutas i.e. the 5 basic elements, Kshiti (Earth), Aap (water), Tej (fire), Marut (air), Vyom (Akash) together are the cause of our sthula Sharira (gross body). Let us analyse scientifically.

Kshiti or Earth is the solid material of our body. Solid gets absorbed in water. So, the next element is water or Aap. Water gets absorbed in fire. Now the next element is fire. Similarly, fire gets absorbed in air. Finally, air gets absorbed in Akash. In this order, the 5 elements coordinate with each other to form our gross body. So, our body is formed from the basic material known as Bhuta. These basic materials have the sequence such as Akash, Vayu, Tej, Aap and Kshiti (Earth) during the formation process. This process is known as Panchikaran. We will describe Panchikaran later in this text.

This gross body is filled with filth, like urine and faecal matter. These have a very bad odour, and no one likes these materials. Since our body possesses all these despicable matters, we need to abandon this. Our body does not deserve to be attached by us. When we really understand our body, we will surely look for a path to get rid of our body and stay at a higher level and perform more and more Purushartha to elevate ourselves.

This gross body is produced due to the karmas that we performed in our past life. Due to a process called Panchikaran, our gross body took shape. In our waking state, we get the experience of the gross objects.

WHAT IS PANCHIKARAN:

The 5 basic elements that we described earlier: Earth, water, fire, air, and Akash first originate in a subtle form. Then by the wish of God, the creator, these 5 elements are divided into three-fold or five-fold, and then each of them is split into 5 parts. Adishankar speaks of this method of formation of the gross body. It is stated as, "Each of these 5 elements is divided into 2 equal parts. While one part is reserved for the element, the other part is again divided into 4 parts and combined with each of the rest. This process is called Panchikaran."

Hence, by this combination of one another's elements, the gross elements like the Earth, water, fire, etc., have taken part in the formation of this gross body.

The features of the gross body are birth, old age, and death. This body can be weak, strong, or stout. This body undergoes many activities during the lifetime. The body has the 5 sense organs, the ear, the skin, etc., through which it enjoys. But all the enjoyments are known as worldly enjoyment, which are transitory in nature and give pains and sorrows eventually.

We have 3 main states known as Avastha. These are known as the waking, dream, and the dreamless sleep or the slumber state.

WAKING STATE:

In the waking state, the soul identifying itself with the body enjoys the taste, smell, women, fragrant articles, respect through garlanding et al. So only the body gets importance in the waking state. By enjoying the external objects, the soul gets both pleasure and pain. Let us describe these 3 states one by one.

DREAM STATE:

In the dream state, the gross body is detached from the mind. The memory does not have any reflection. Hence, in this state, our body does not get any pleasure arising out of the dream. However, our desires form an imaginative gross body. All animate and divine beings that are experienced by our mind during this state do not pertain to our own body. So basically, our gross body gets its importance during the awakened state only.

SLUMBER OR DREAMLESS SLEEP STATE:

The mind does not work here. The body is dormant. The intellect, memory, and ego do not work. It is only the breath that works in our body. So, in this state, our gross body also does not get any importance.

Now let us discuss the 2 more Shariras: Sukshma (subtle) and the Karan (causal) Sharira or body.

SUKSHMA (SUBTLE SHARIRA):

The Sukshma Sharira comprises of the following:

1. The 5 Karmendriyas: We have the 5 motor nerves that operate (after receiving directives from our brains); the Karmendriyas that are responsible for actions such as speech, work, walk, urine excretion, and excretion of faeces. These actions are done by the Karmendriyas such as the organ of speech, the hands, the legs, the urinogenital organ, and the anus respectively.

2. The 5 Jnanendriyas: We have the 5 sensory organs that operate (after receiving directives from the brain); the Jnanendriyas that are responsible for hearing, touching, seeing, tasting, and smelling, such as the ears, the skin, the eyes, the tongue, and the nose, respectively.

3. The 5 Vayus (air): Prana, Apana, Udana, Samana, and Vyana are the 5 Vayus or air flowing in our body. Without the Prana and the Apana Vayu, we cannot live. We have already discussed in detail about these Vayus earlier.

4. The 5 basic elements or the Pancha Bhutas: We have discussed the Pancha Bhutas earlier.

5. Buddhi (Intellect), Avidya (ignorance), Kama (attachment), and karma (work with the desire to have results).

6. Manas (mind) and Ahamkara (ego) and Chitta (memory cells).

All of the above comprise the Sukshma Sharira or our subtle body.

This Sthula Sharira is also known as the Linga Sharira because all the elements thereof are insentient. They need a driver and a limb to translate the directives of the Jivatma to perform tasks. Say, smell is insentient unless recognised by the Jivatma and not acted upon by the limbs, say the noses. Because of this reason, we call the Sthula Sharira the Linga Sharira also.

KARANA SHARIRA (CAUSAL BODY):

We have understood that the gross body and the subtle body are not real. The bodies meet their death one day or another. They are not the Atman. So, they are stated to be the Anatman. Now, who is the cause of this creation is the causal body or the Karana Sharira.

Earlier, we have already discussed that the Jivatma is there in the body. Near the Jivatma, the Brahman is seated. The Brahman does not act, and the Jivatma acts. This being clear, now we must understand who created the gross and the subtle bodies.

If you remember, we have stated that God or the Brahman is not visible to the Jivatma because He is veiled by His own illusory power. This illusory power is known as maya. Maya creates all this. Maya is known as Avyakta. It operates with the 3 Gunas, Sat Guna, Rajas Guna, and Tamas Guna. This maya or the illusory power of God is the cause of all creations and is the Karan Sharira (Causal Body). When we say, body, it means it is not permanent. Everyone from a morsel to the Brahman is subject to death.

As the Jivatma understands Pram Atman and performs Purushartha through this body, with a very strong yearning for liberation, the veil of maya will no longer exist, and the human being will be elevated to attain salvation (in this birth), i.e. the spiritual aspirant will attain ultimate freedom by the grace of God.

Now before we go through the meditation processes in detail, let me give a detailed list of the characteristics of Sat, Rajas, and Tamas Gunas so that the reader is aware of these Gunas, which are the basic characteristics of maya.

We say, 'Triguna Rahitam': - meaning thereby, beyond all the 3 Gunas. And God is Triguna Rahitam. God is beyond all the 3 Gunas (Sat, Rajas, and Tamas).

CHARACTERISTICS OF PEOPLE WITH SAT GUNA:

Humility, modesty, non-injury, patience, uprightness, service to the teacher, steadfastness, respect for the Guru, purity, self-control, absence of attachment to the sense objects; perception of evil in birth, death, old age, sickness, and pain. A Sat Guni does not have an iota of ego. He/she is not attached to children, wife, wealth, home, or to any tangible or intangible objects that bind. He/she is established in yoga, and does not have any love for society. He/she loves solitary places. These people have a strong yearning for liberation and they perform Purushartha to meet God in the present life. All these characteristics are stated in the Bhagavad Gita.

CHARACTERISTICS OF RAJAS GUNA:

The people with Rajas Guna basically have greed, avarice, attachment to worldly objects, a luxurious lifestyle, and a desire for fruitive work.

These people pray to God, but they do not resort to the processes of Soul Elevation. They die before knowing their Own Self. As a result of this, these people fall into the repeated cycles of birth and death. Since they have not tried to know their Self, they may not get a human birth in their next birth.

CHARACTERISTICS OF TAMAS GUNA:

Laziness, procrastination, involvement in speculative activities, having friendships with bad people, doing harm to society as a whole, and many such undesirable characteristics are present in people with Tamas Guna.

These people can make themselves better by resorting to the processes of listening, reflecting, and meditating (Shravan, Manan, and Nididhyasana).

When a human being has a very clear understanding of God and His characteristics, when Jivatma turns to Param Brahman, and from there on, the yogi resorts to meditation to know God.

NOTE: After gaining some knowledge about the Brahman, about our body, and about the various Gunas, let us now concentrate on spirituality.

There is a Sanskrit mantra:

"Dhyanavasthita-tad-gaten Manasa Pasyanti Yam Yoginah...": -

Yogis see You (God) in their minds through meditation!

When we discuss more on spirituality to have a better understanding, we need to refer to the scriptures that directly deal with this topic. Almost all Vedantas (Upanishads) discuss spirituality thoroughly.

What are these Upanishads or the Vedantas! Basically, Vedanta means the end part of the Vedas. Upanishad means 'let us sit and talk together.' You will see that these scriptures discuss the Brahman and the Atman (Super Soul and soul) either through various discussions, for example, the son talking to his father or a disciple discussing his doubts and clarifying those doubts with God-realised Saints/Gurus. As we discussed the dialogue held between Yama Raj and Nachiketa on Brahman and how to know it and be free.

DISCUSSION BETWEEN SAINT NIDAGH AND HIS FATHER RUBHU:

To go deeper, let us detail the discussions between Nidagh and his father, the great saint namely Rubhu.

From childhood, Nidagh was a spiritual aspirant. He took permission from his father Rubhu and went on a pilgrimage. He bathed in many holy rivers and seas, experiencing much during his journey. Finally, he returned and shared his feelings with his father. He said, "My dear father! After bathing in numerous holy places, I have accumulated many good deeds and concluded that this world is transitory. It is subject to destruction one day. In this world, everything is created and destroyed. In fact, these materials, destined for destruction, are repeatedly created. At that time, the ardent efforts and creative activities of living beings become unstable. These beings have very short lifespans. All these wealth-related materials are sources of demolition or destruction. This wealth, leading to demise, is like iron nails. Our mind acts as a magnet for this wealth and collects it. This attachment of our mind to wealth is strong. Like a traveller becoming dispassionate passing through a desert, I am also becoming dispassionate towards worldly objects. I feel that these objects are sources of pain and suffering. The thought of how to rid myself of these worldly objects always lingers in my mind. I know that all this wealth will grow and become abundant one day, but I believe this abundance will not bring me happiness. Spouse and children are also sources of suffering for me. Even Goddess Lakshmi, who is delicate and merciful, creates attachment. I am certain that living beings cannot find happiness from Goddess Lakshmi, the giver of all wealth. Just as a drop of water on a leaf blade is temporary, the lifespan of living beings is temporary. Because of this, I am contemplating leaving the world like a madman. Worldly objects are like poisonous snakes that thoroughly digest living beings, preventing them from realising their true selves. All these human beings are burdened with worldly sufferings."

It is possible for the air to enclose our whole body. It is also possible that the sky may break and the seawater may thicken. But it is not possible on my part to depend on this fleeting life. For me, as I believe; 'Life is, that where we can get the objects needed by us properly, and to get that we do not have to lament. Further, one experiences supreme peace after getting the object.' The trees and birds also have life. So, there is nothing great to have a life. But the human beings who resort to analysis of the self (Atma Chintan) are said to be leading their lives on the proper path. From these human beings who could make it not to return and fall into the repeated cycles of birth and death are adjudged to be the best of all. The human beings who lead their life till their death having attained senility without realising the self-have a life very similar to that of the life of a donkey. They become bound to carry the burden of the world like the donkey.

BAD EFFECTS OF EGO:

For the wise, the scriptures are like a burden. A person free from attachment and aversion, for him knowledge is a burden. The persons who are attached, they have no peace, their minds are burdens for them. Ego is the cause of all sorrows. Ego leads to damaging ends. Ego leads to wicked mental disorder and desires sprout thereof. This is why ego is the worst enemy of human beings. No other enemies are better than ego in human beings. Whatever luxuries I enjoyed owing to satisfying my ego, all those luxuries were false. A life without ego is an accomplished one.

MENTAL VIBRATION (CHITTA VRITTI):

Our mind is wandering without any fruitful achievements because we are controlled by our anxieties. The human being wanders aimlessly from far to near places like a dog. Under the control of my mental vibrations (Chitta Vritti) arising out of the mirage of desires which is like a bitch, I was also wandering from place to place like a dog following this bitch of desires. But I am now fully freed from the shackles of this desire-like bitch arising out of my Chitta Vritti. It is very difficult to control the mind (Chitta Nigraha). Rather, it is comparatively easier to uproot the Sumeru (the sacred five-peak mountain of the Hindus and other religions like the Jains and the Buddhists) and it is easier to drink all the water of a sea, but to control the mind is next to impossible. Chitta accepts the external and internal information. The 3 states (Jagrat-awaken, Swapna-dream, and Sushupti-slumber) of the world depend on the Chitta Vritti only. Chitta or our mind is subtler than the world. And hence, knowing this, we should try our best to control our mind.

EFFECS OF DESIRE:

Now Nidagh is talking about the effects of desire on him to his father, Saint Rubhu. He says, "As a wicked mouse cuts the strings of a violin asunder, in the same way my desires are spoiling my best qualities. Again, he compares the desire to a monkey who dares jump from trees to trees, though jumping lofty trees courage. Nidagh says that my desires are also daring to reach places which are usually not treaded by the wise. Though I have already satisfied my desires several times, still I am not stopping there and continuously having new desires and running and jumping on various objectives to satisfy my new desires. So where is the end! Because of this desire, my mind is moving to the sky in a moment and in the next moment it is going much below the Earth's crust. In some other moment my mind is wandering from countries to countries. If you judge all the sorrows of this world, then this desire gives us the worst sufferings and not only that, but this desire also gives pain to my neighbours. The desire is like an epidemic. The persons who have shunned the thought of desires and not given way to the desires, such people have duly destroyed the desires. If we leave the thoughts for a moment, we will get extreme happiness. If we have a small amount of thought waves in our mind, then also we will get sorrowfulness."

OUR BODY IS NOT IMPORTANT:

Nidagh talks about the unimportance of our body. He said, "There is nothing inferior to this body. This body has no good qualities in it. This body is extremely bad and unpleasant. In this great house-like body, an owner full of ego is residing. I do not bother even if this body desires to live for an indefinite period or if this body gets destroyed within a small span of time. I am not at all interested in this house-like body because animal-like Indriyas are residing in it. Not only that, in the yard of this body, a desire-like monkey is moving, and slaves like the mind and the memory, etc., are also present here. Again, in this body, the mouth cavity looks quite ferocious because the monkey-like tongue affects it by opening the bone-like teeth at first."

These are precisely the reasons why I do not like this body. This body is covered by flesh and blood both internally and externally. So, how can this mortal body look beautiful? One should not doubt the consistency of this body, if it is believed that the lightning is not dynamic or if it is believed that the city of the angels is calm and quiet.

All the 3 stages of human life are full of fear. When we are a child, we fear our parents and also fear children who are older than us. When we are young, we are caught in the nets of lust that lurk in our minds. Because of this lust or the desire for the opposite sex, we are defeated most of the time. We totter as we become old. Looking at them, our spouse, relatives, offspring, and even the servants mock us. Our desire grows in old age due to our increasing incapabilities. Due to senility, our hearts move towards an end. The happiness that worldly people seek, they never attain. Time is very powerful. It has the capability to convert small grasses and dust into royal emperors and can also turn large mountains like Sumeru into gold. Time has the power to bring sorrows to everyone and devours all. Time pervades the Trilokas (The Heaven, the Earth, and The Patal).

MEN'S ATTRACTION TOWARDS WOMEN:

This body is as dynamic and as flexible as a machine. What else is present in the bodies of the women which look like toys made of flesh and bones? And why are the women's bodies stated to be so beautiful? What is present inside the eyes of a woman other than skin, flesh, blood, and tears which are believed to be attractive? If there is nothing tangible or interesting there, then why are we so endeared by the body of a woman? We know that women are as fickle as the water of the Ganges that flows cheerfully from high mountains such as Sumeru, and women adorn themselves with dazzling necklaces of pearls. The same women, when they eventually die due to the cruelty of time, have their corpses' breasts licked by jackals in the graveyards. A woman becomes lovable when she maintains a nice hairstyle and adorns herself with good ornaments and various attractive outfits. But with sorrow, I declare that after the death of a lady, it becomes very difficult to touch her corpse. What is this attachment for? What is this attraction for? All seems to be delusion to me. Nidagh further states about women, "When the corpses of these women are burnt in the pyre of the graveyards, it seems as if they are the sinful deeds of the creator Brahma (Brahma is known as the God who creates, Vishnu is the maintainer, and Lord Shiva is the annihilator). Though there is simplicity present in women, they are filled with insipidity. Here the hunter is compared with the desire for sex. The nets are compared with women, and the deer are compared with men. These men are ready to be bound by the nets of desire for sex with women. Further, the mind of men is compared with mud, whereas men are compared with fishes. The bodies of the ladies are bound by the lustful string of desire. This string is dragging the fish-like men into the muds of the mind. Now you can well understand the fate of the men who are attracted towards women owing to the muddy thoughts of their minds. The sea is the creator of all these flawed pearls. A person having a wife is indulged in the desire for luxuries. But a man who is not married, for such a person, there is no reason to enjoy and get indulged in luxuries. A person who has shunned a wife by not marrying, such a human being has verily given up the world. He has become happy. This is why I want the tether of sorrows to remain away from me."

THE WORLD IS SUBJECT TO DEMOLITION:

Nidagh further stated that this world is subject to demolition. When this world vanishes, at that time the directions are not visible. The lands, states, and countries get dissolved by the onslaught of time. The mountains break into pieces, and the stars also fall, having broken down into smaller parts. The oceans and the seas have no water. The pole star becomes invisible. The demons meet their ends. The great siddhas also fall into the shackles of death. Lord Vishnu, who has neither birth nor death, disappears along with Lord Brahma. We know that Lord Brahma is the creator who is also created by Lord Vishnu. As water runs into Badabanala (It is the name of the fire inside the seas or inside the oceans); in the same manner, all the living beings (men, women, animals, birds, worms, insects) run towards death. At that time, all things that were plentiful become scarce. In a moment, all things enter a state of danger. In a moment, all wealth is available. In the flick of a second, there is the existence of life, and in another moment, there is death and destruction. All these illusory things/materials/lives are subject to destruction. Here, the courageous and victorious are annihilated by the timid. Hundreds can be killed by a single individual. This way such oddities are prevalent all over. The oddities that arise due to the desires of our minds convert into poisons at length. Do you know, the poison is not that dreadful. It destroys the present living beings. But the desires for the world and the worldly luxuries have the capabilities to destroy births after births. My whole mind is fully burnt in the desire-like Davanala (The huge fire that burns a forest completely is called Davanala). Standing in the mirage of a desert, I am far from the enjoyment of worldly luxuries.

Nidagh seeks help of his erudite father, Saint Rubhu. He says, "Oh, my dear father! Oh, my dear Guru! Please tell me the philosophies (Tattva Jnana) concerning Spiritual Knowledge. Or else, I will silently shun my fish-like mind and think of God to get His blessings."

SAINT RUBHU ANSWERS:

Saint Rubhu says, "My dear son! You have become the best among the wise. You have nothing so important for you to know. God's blessings have showered on you and for this reason, you have become the knower of everything by the application of your own intelligence and by the power of internal analysis. However, I will clean up the pollutants that are still existing in your mind. Sama (already discussed about Sama earlier i.e. disciplined concentration of the mind on the goal), Vichar (Internal analysis of good thoughts), Santosh (Satisfaction) and Satsang (To be with God, to be with the association of the wise and the erudite, to read the scriptures with deep concentration and internal analysis) are the doorways to achieve God. If one among these qualities is adopted also, then a person achieves the other 3 qualities automatically. If you want to get away from this world and achieve the ultimate freedom, then study of the scriptures, practise penance or asceticism, adopt Dama (Control of the sense organs-already discussed before) with sincere efforts and get involved in Satsang. These are to be practised to increase one's own wisdom. Self-introspection sprouts in one's own self, by virtue of your own experience, by listening and continuously practising the advice of the Guru. In addition to this one must constantly keep the various proofs stated in the scriptures. If you have given up the desires and all inquiries of various hopes, then attaining solitude leading to God becomes automatic. When the mastery of the mind ceases, then we say that Chitta Vritti is fully quelled. This is known as Chitta Vritti Nirodha (Nirodha means stoppage). This state is known as Kaivalya or Parashanti (Parashanti means supreme peace). First, you should completely give up your thoughts of all worldly objects as the self and remain as if you are deaf and dumb. Vision of discrimination as stated in various words leads to delusion and becomes fruitless. Oneness; devoid of the beginning, the middle and end; is very bright etc. words become a barrier to institute self-analysis (Atma Tattva). All these manifestations are Om or Pranav. Whatever becomes visible, is verily obvious in the universe of our minds. A part of the mental vibration (Chitta Vritti) is what we see. Hence, the mind is everything. You can perform all the worldly activities and still with the knowledge of the oneness of the Atman by the application of your mind, be peaceful like the ocean and be steadfast in your mind. You can get your own welfare by the performance of this activity."

FEELING OF NON-OWNERSHIP:

Think that desire is like dry grass. Atma Jnana (Knowledge of the Self) is like a fire. It verily burns the desire into ashes. Samadhi (The state of deep contemplation) is not achieved by remaining silent. Wherever a jewel lies, irrespective of its placement, a worldly person gets attracted towards it. In the same logic, the whole universe is attracted towards the Para-Tattva (The Supreme Brahman). This Atman has both ownership and non-ownership. When desire is not present, Atman does not assert its ownership of anything. But as it goes near desires, it asserts its ownership. One can experience both characteristics of ownership and non-ownership in Brahman. Where you find such marvellousness, take its shelter. "I am not the owner," when this thought is fully established in the mind, then only undeterred supreme equality remains as its residue. In this state of mind, you become one with God. The whole world becomes quite illusive for you. Human beings are said to have good qualities if and only if they are established in Sat Guna (We have described Sat Guna earlier). These human beings remain ever happy like the Moon and are progressive in their nature.

ESSENTIAL QUALITIES OF A SPIRITUAL ASPIRANT:

By this time, we have already understood about Sampatti and Vipatti. Goodness can be attributed to the day, and badness is attributed to the night. So, if someone is established in Atma Tattva, then they do not get scared by forsaking a golden lotus because such wealth leads to Vipatti eventually. The wise are well satisfied with the pleasure that is available with ease. These people do not desire other materials. They lead their life as ordained in the scriptures. These spiritual aspirants are adorned with qualities like Maitri, Karuna, Mudita, and Upeksha.

Let us understand these qualities:

- Maitri: Friendliness towards people who are happy.

- Karuna: Compassion towards those who suffer.

- Mudita: Sympathetic joy towards the virtuous.

- Upeksha: Sympathy or indifference towards the wrongdoers.

All these aspirants stay in equilibrium of mind, have equanimity, and manage their livelihood with honesty. These people remain beyond dignity. They have highly expanded and merciful hearts like that of the great ocean. They travel on the right path like the path traversed by the Sun. They have their original thought process and they go as per their own decisions. They also carefully analyse by using their own wisdom on the creation of the world, which is illusive and transitory in nature. They never get involved in fruitless work and remain away from the wicked. Death devours all; knowing this, they never ignore this truth. If they need to ignore, then they do so for the body, the bones, the flesh, the blood, and the likes which are transitory by nature. They verily observe the Chidatma (the Supreme Spirit) in everyone that is duly hung as beads in a single garland, which is the Brahman. They leave the useless and adopt what is useful. They have the full conviction that the basic characteristics of the mind are to move out and it has no interest to remain inside. By their own experience and by the advice given by the Gurus plus what is stated in the scriptures, these aspirants know that, 'I am the Brahman.' After having such a strong feeling, they give up unhappiness.

These people develop tolerance so that they do not feel the heat of the fire. The fire does not affect these aspirants. They feel the smearing of the charcoal dust as an anointment of sandalwood paste on them. Basically, they do not find a difference between charcoal powder vis-a-vis sandalwood paste. They remain happy in all circumstances. If they are pierced with arrows also, they feel the pain as if it is calming them as cold water calms the heat of the Sun in summer. So, pain and pleasure are one and the same for these people. If beheaded, they feel to have attained sleep with happiness. They feel extremely happy when they remain silent or when they behave as if they are not able to speak nor are able to talk. Both deafness and dumbness are welcome for them because by that they feel happiness being in such states. In this state of mind, hundreds of harmful attacks of the sword give a feeling like the heating of delicate lotus petals on them. This state of mind is not attained by ignorance. This state of mind is sprouted from Atma Jnana which is a result of vairagya (dispassion). Advice of the Guru, knowledge of the scriptures, and one's own experience purify the mind. By this, it is possible to meet or realise the Atman (Atma Sakshatkar) every moment. When confusion ends, the knowledge of the various directions becomes clear. In the same manner, with pure intellect, the unreal world is annihilated. Friends and relatives, wealth, our own children cannot do an iota of benefit for us. If the physical pain is over from our body, then also we do not get any benefits towards getting Atma Jnana. In the same logic, by traversing and taking a bath in various holy places also, God realisation is not possible at all. The aspirant can get the Supreme Abode being in the pure intellect.

A SPIRITUAL ASPIRANT (YOGI) REMAINS IN PEACE:

As the sunlight destroys darkness, similarly a spiritual aspirant remains in peace in all worldly situations such as sorrow, thirst, and longing. A yogi having the characteristics of mind control (Sama) is believed by both the mild and the cruel persons. We know that Goddess Mahalakshmi bestows wealth and prosperity. The peace and tranquillity that are available to a yogi are much better than the embrace of Goddess Mahalakshmi. Similarly, a yogi feels more peaceful even after he is fed with elixir (Amrit). A yogi is said to be in peace if he neither feels happy nor sorry in situations like hunger or no hunger. If the yogi is not perturbed both in war or in peace; in different festivities, and in death, he is said to be in peace. These persons are as clean as the Moon. A yogi duly established in Sama is loved and respected by sages who perform Yagnas. They are also respected by the Saints, the wise who are well-versed in all the Vedas (Shrotriya), the kings, the sadhus, and the sadhus who live in jungles. A yogi becomes qualified for Atma Jnana if he drinks the nectar of satisfaction and is very peaceful. These yogis achieve unison with the Supreme eventually in this birth. The yogis remain well balanced even after getting much wealth. They have no greed for materials that are not available to them. They have the same behaviour in situations of happiness and sorrowfulness. These aspirants are called to be 'satisfied.' Remaining very satisfied with whatever is available or not available can be compared with a Sadhwi who feels quite happy remaining within the premises of her house. Jivan Mukta (to be described in detail later) is one of the characteristics when in all circumstances, a yogi remains happy and peaceful. Such a yogi is said to be in the state of Jivan Mukta. When all dualities are absent, peace ensues immediately. (Dualities means sorrowfulness-happiness, hot-cold, brightness and darkness, and the likes).

The yogis try their best to attain various Satsangas until they have not made the Atman duly rested. Our Atman is in a state of instability owing to the continuous kicks by the breath-in and breath-out cycles. The yogi is determined to seek the ultimate truth, and that is why he practices calmness of the mind. In the mind control methodology, Pranayama is also practised under the active guidance of a realised Guru. Pranamaya Kosha and Annamaya Kosha are complementary to each other. If one sheath is controlled, the other sheath is controlled automatically. We can take the example of the axle and the wheels of a moving bullock cart. If the wheel stops, then the axle does not rotate, and vice versa. It means when the axle is also made to stop, then the wheels, which are moving due to the association of the axle, will stop. So, either resorting to Pranayama or mind control methodologies, the objectives of Sama are satisfied. The yogi can seek higher spiritual levels.

We have already stated that there are 3 Avastha: the awakened state, the dream state, and the slumber state. Apart from these 3 states, there is another state known as Turiya Avastha. In this conscious state, there is utter silence of the yogi for a prolonged period. Here, silence is predominant with the yogi. If the yogi is resting in this state, being completely free from worldly affairs, then even if the yogi is maintaining a family, staying alone, or resorting to sannyasa; his intellect, memory, ego, and mind will not get confused. He can reach God. He is in a state equal to a wave-less ocean. Many of us think that a yogi means a person who stays in a jungle or in any secluded place away from society. But it is not the truth. A yogi established in Dispassion, Sama, Dama, Uparati, Titiksha, Shraddha, Samadhan having an ardent yearning for liberation, he may be maintaining a family or not, he can elevate his own soul beyond doubts. An iota of desire brings the yogi down. If desire sprouts by chance, then the yogi must restart his Purushartha. This is why seers say that the process of realisation of the Super Soul is like walking on a sword.

When the yogi feels others as himself, when he has empathy, when he feels the pains of others based on situations, then there is no discrimination among the souls present in entities. This feeling is called Vishwatma.

All the living and non-living beings are annihilated during Pralaya as the dream is fully absorbed in slumber. The wise and the erudite identify this soul as Param Atman, Yajna, or the ultimate truth.

A bangle made of gold has no separate existence than gold and in the same way the various worlds created by God are no different from God or the Param Atma or the Brahman. God has created an illusion by having the various objects of creation and shown to all others as different from one another. And that is why we see the differences which are not the truth. God is all-pervasive and is seated in the heart of hearts of all entities. A seer visualises the same God in all entities.

When the beholder gets absorbed in the creation, they become bound. If the beholder does not see the difference in the various entities of this world, then only they become free. All shackles are opened, and salvation is achieved.

The feeling of 'me and mine' creates the difference. These are known as Darshan and the beholder is termed as Drashta. All the scenes of the world are transitory, but the mind which makes and breaks the desires becomes bound to these objects. So, only he/she moves far away from realising the self and, hence realising God. Until the desires of the mind are not stopped completely, until that time, the path to freedom is not visible. Many seers say, "when the door to the world is closed, then only the spiritual door gets opened." Though we must elevate our own souls by our own souls, still an agent or a guide, namely Guru's active guidance, is necessary to perform Purushartha.

Note: Guru: A person well-versed in the 4 Vedas (Rik, Yajur, Sama, and Atharv), and having a great heart, sinless, very calm, and fully satisfied (As a fire becomes calm and fully satisfied after fully devouring the fuel) is termed as a Guru. Additionally, from the moment a disciple accosts the Guru and begs for spiritual guidance, he becomes his/her friend from that moment.

The whole universe is Manomaya because the mind sees everything from its own angle of vision. Lord Brahma, being an agent of the Lord, has created the universe by using his mental imaginations. 'Anything created is subject to annihilation eventually.' Lord Brahma is also created by the Brahman. So, only Lord Brahma must meet his death at the proper time. The mind is not established in the pure Brahman, neither externally nor internally. If someone asks you who is this 'mind,' the answer is Sankalp or desire. We say, "Sankalp Vikalpatmaka Manah." This means the mind desires and reverses the desires. The mind vibrates (Chitta Vritti) owing to the desire waves. When these waves are stopped, the mind will tend to move inward and from there on tries to reach God. No one could be able to separate desire from the mind. When all desires are stopped, then the brilliant Self (Atma) becomes obvious. 'Vishwa, I, you' all these words narrate differences. When everything is one, then these words are meaningless. The oneness is the Brahman. During Maha-Pralay, nothing will be seen. All will be annihilated other than the pure Atma. This Atma is like the Sun, and this Atma never sets. The Atma is divine. Speeches cannot reach the Atma. The speech returns thereafter without reaching the Atma. This Atma is the doer of all. It is also all-knowing. This is free and is the 'Purush.' What we imagine about the Atman and its shape, He is shapeless. He is infinite. He is the 'Akalpaniya' (beyond all imaginations) Brahman. He is Purushottama.

DESCRIPTION AKASH:

Akash (ether) is of 3 types: Chittakash, Chidakash, and Bhoutika Akash. Out of these 3, Chidakash is the subtlest of all. When the person moves from one place to the other, the Chittakash differs, but the residue which remains is Chidakash. When the existence of Chidakash is no longer felt, then only the path to getting God becomes achievable. When the yogi, by dint of extreme dispassion and mercifulness, establishes Chidakash with due cheerfulness, the state that the yogi obtains is known as Samadhi. In this state, the yogi has no anger, nor has an iota of aversion. All creations are absent in this state of mind. During this practice, the yogi acquires the power to move to any places in the universe. The yogi does not visualise anything externally. This invisibility is termed as 'Jnana.' This Avastha is known as Kaivalya (Oneness). This is known as the desired knowledge of Chidatmaka. All the scenes, which are nothing but illusion, move out of the mind of the yogi. He experiences pure Atma. The whole world seems to be false. It is like a mosquito fighting with a lion in the cave: which has no truth. Or it is like binding a mad elephant in the hole of a corner: which is false.

When the mind thinks of the body, at that time the Atman becomes attracted to the body. When all desires stop, the Atman does not involve itself in any Dharma whatsoever. This mind is changing everything. It changes a Kalp (thousands of years) to a moment and vice versa.

After narrating these philosophies, Saint Rubhu says, "In my opinion, the world is the imagination of the mind."

YOGI SAYS I AM THE BRAHMAN!

If a person lacks peacefulness and concentration, and dispassion has not touched him, then such a person cannot have Self-realisation. The knowledge of high-quality Kaivalya, a person should practise mental solitude for a long period of time to be with God. The disturbed mind cannot enquire into the self. A person never fears when he sees God (Who is beyond all qualities, the absolute truth, owner of all minds, beyond all dualities, and blissful) and in himself. The yogi feels Brahman in himself and speaks thus, "I am the Brahman. All the demigods, the angels, the demons, the nagas, the vasus pray to me." Brahman is greater than the greatest; higher than the highest. He is constant and unending; has no beginning and no end. He is the creator, the maintainer, and the destroyer. All worlds are like beads of a garland hanging on me. He is engaged in the welfare of everyone and everything. God is super brilliant. Brahman is Omnipotent, Omnipresent and Omniscient. Brahman is Sanatan and the Puran Purush (the Oldest being). This feeling in a yogi about the Brahman makes him elevated. Such spiritual aspirants can go beyond all activities to realise the Brahman. They are free and fearless.

Attachment is the cause of bondage. A person is free when he has left or given up physically and mentally all sorts of attachments. We desire and give up desire; we imagine and again enter reality; we visualise and do not visualise – all these are the creations of God. All imaginations are from God. This whole universe is the imagination of God. The various energies of God perform. God is immobile and yet He is sentient. He is all-merciful and impartial.

The yoga as detailed through Tri-Nachiketagni in the Kathopanishad path to attaining the Brahman. The yoga and the Jnana as detailed in the Swetaswatara Upanishad also are not the path to the Brahman. Starting from Kapil Muni to the great saint Charvak, all the Samkhya Yogas and their processes do not lead to the Brahman. And this is why a spiritual aspirant should not let their mind be confused in debating over the topics of Jiva and Param (Soul and the Super Soul). The yogi should instead be established in the remembrance of God and His qualities and His philosophies to rise in the rung of Soul Elevation and thereby meet God eventually.

When the yogi becomes very decisive and has the conviction that the mind is the universe, then we can say that he is with true wisdom. We know that the mind desires and rewinds its own desires after some time. These are only because of our Chitta Vritti. The yogi whose mind is fixed and undeterred by Chitta Vritti, Brahma, Vishnu, and Maheshwara. Giving up all objects is rare, and still rarer is getting the Tattva Jnana. By this knowledge, the yogi verily enters a state or Avastha known as Sahaj Avastha in the Vedas. Until the yogi finds a difference, fear does not completely leave his mind. So, non-discrimination is the key. Oneness is the key. Recognising the real and the imaginary is the key. Understanding clearly what is permanent and what is transitory is the key for an accomplished yogi. If there is an ardent desire to meet the ever-blissful Brahman, then the yogi verily meets Him through the eyes of knowledge (Jnana Chakshu). Just as a blind person is not able to see the Sun, in the same manner, a yogi devoid of Jnana Chakshu cannot meet God. Brahman is the source of profound knowledge. He is the knowledge of all knowledges. The characteristic of truth is also profound knowledge. So, God is the truth. Mortal human beings proceed to eternity by this profound knowledge, i.e. they verily achieve salvation by meeting Brahman. Brahman is the real cause of everything in this universe. A yogi becomes doubtless after meeting Brahman (We call this Brahma Sakshatkar). When the yogi has Brahma Sakshatkar, all his karmas (actions like the performances of Prana karma, Yajna, Tapa, Dana, and the like) are destroyed asunder. We have already stated that Soul Elevation is only possible when there is no existence of karma. By this, the knots of the heart (hridgranthi) get untied or opened.

SAINT RUBHU ADVISES:

O my dear son! Remain ever fearless. Shun the unreal. Get well absorbed in the realisation of the Self. As the vision of water in a mirage inside a desert is not the reality, in the same way, all the 3 Avasthas such as Jagrat, Swapna and Sushupti are not the reality. All these primarily belong to God. So, God is only real. The wise among the wisest; leave all the unreal and become steadfast in the processes of enquiring the self. To know what is real and what is unreal is to be meditated upon. The solution is within us. So, putting our minds outwardly, we need to look inward. Disciplined control of the Indriyas and Antahkaran; giving up all control; verily destroys the various scenes of the world, which are not the truth. Through the ardent tool of Atma Chintan, inching towards realisation of God is possible. Fixity of the mind on the objective, quelling of the Chitta Vritti can only lead to meeting the God. Performance of all these has no match. The Brahman is subtler than the subtlest and is indestructible.

THE EASY WAY TO REALISE GOD:

Saint Rubhu says, "Let me tell you the methods of getting rid of the Chitta Vritti. First of all, determine what the various objects are that disturb your mind. Stop thinking and reflecting on these objects. A yogi who dislikes giving up the various objects, does not pursue loneliness, and does not agree with the subordination of the Self; such yogis can well deserve to be visualised as the most hated worms. The best way to find peace is to give up what you like the most through your own careful efforts. There is no better way than this. When the desireless scissors cut the mind asunder, thereafter the all-knower Brahman is available to the yogi always. This is why the yogi is supposed to maintain a consistently desireless state. Eventually, the yogi should let go of all the Chitta Vritti (that verily lead to the unreal world) and become very intelligent by establishing his mind in the pure Brahman (Param Atma is pure and the truth)."

Meditate upon the heart by embracing extreme dispassion and constant practice of establishing the mind in the Shuddha Brahma without an iota of wavering of the mind. Even a ripple of vibration of the mind can get the yogi away from realisation of God. You must have seen ripples getting created in still water when a paper rider is thrown on it. Chitta Vritti creates thought waves which are like ripples on water. Creation of these ripples is to stop; meaning thereby, 'the mind is goaded by the yogi so that no Chitta Vritti is created.' Maharshi Patanjali in his work, Ashtanga Yoga, writes, "Yoga is that which stops the Chitta Vritti (Yogas Chitta Vritti Nirodhah)." Willpower is one of the characteristics of the mind. This willpower is used as a sword. It is used to slay all the thought waves. In this situation, all the fears of the mind are also vanished. All the other vices such as greed, attachment, anger etc. will be tethered by this willpower. The yogi becomes steadfast and remains one-pointed without wavering of his mind. When this mind is seen nowhere! When the basic feelings of 'me', 'mine', 'yours' are vanished fully. The yogi is now in a mindless state. Mind desires. If the mind is not there, the desire has no existence. As during autumn, the various pieces of clouds that float in the sky are blown away by the obstruction of air; in the same way, by the pure thoughts, the mind gets obstructed and finds no place to exist. Param Purusha is having no mind and that is why He never gets disturbed if all the water of the oceans rain after being converted to steam. In the same manner, if during Pralay, all the 49 Vayus flow vigorously or if all the Dwadasa Adityas (The 12 Adityas are known as Dwadasa Adityas) emit warmth, then also the Purusha never gets perturbed. The Purusha is steadfast as usual. In the same way, when the mind is not there, the yogi is also steadfast. When you meditate for a prolonged time say for hours, then the state that you attend is devoid of all mental vibrations. This state is the state of conscious slumber or Samadhi. In the state of Samadhi, the yogi is very much aware and concentrated on the creator only.

The Sadhaka becomes perfect or is termed as a siddha when the mind is destroyed by the performance of such Purushartha. So, my dear son, get fully absorbed in the 'state of desirelessness'.

As the characteristic of fire is warmth, similarly fickleness is the characteristic of the mind. Know that this is the transitory world. The mind that is devoid of fickleness is like nectar. The shastras call this nectar Moksha.

The fickleness of the mind is Avidya or ignorance. Ignorance is the cause of all sorrows. 'To have' and 'not to have' arise from this Avidya. These desires are our enemies. The dutiful need to take utmost care in not giving way to the desires.

O my dear son! When the objective is clear, it becomes easier to achieve. You need to resort to Nirvikalpa Samadhi by deploying your desireless mind on the objective. Nirvikalpa means that which has no alternative. So, you have no other alternatives to get to your objective. You need to subjugate your mind with your own mind-only and remain away from woe, pain, agony, and sorrows. Then only you can find peace. The mind that has real detachment from the worldly objects can oppose the mind that is otherwise attracted by worldly pleasure. Any king who is established on his throne can defeat any other king/s to secure his own throne and succeed. Any person who is still a slave to his own desires is verily fallen in the whirlpool of the world's ocean and cannot rescue themselves to get back to the brink safely. Shun all desires and attachments. They undoubtedly bind you. So, what can rescue you as a boat in this world's ocean? It is the mind that has no desires, no vibrations, and no attachments. Dear Nidagh! Cut all the mental vibrations into very small parts with your strong mind that has already shunned all temptations of the Indriyas. Nothing of this world can disturb the self-disciplined mind now. This strong mind will work as the raft to rescue you from the world's ocean. Please remember, it is only you yourself who can take you from one brink of the ocean to the other, and no one else can help you get rid of this world's ocean where you are drowned. When the mind of our own Antahkaran is projected towards worldly desires, at that time, we should be able to recognise the state of the mind and retract it from projecting out and swerving away from the achievement of our own objectives of meeting with the ever-blissful Brahman. This polluted mind, being forsaken by the yogi, peace ensues immediately, and all the mental vibrations get subdued.

SEQUENCING THE VARIOUS ACTIVITIES TO QUELL CHITTA VRITTI:

This is to be taken as an exercise. We should go step by step. First, recognise the various desires. Retract the various elements of Antahkaran towards the objective starting from manas or mind. The intellect and the ego must follow the path.

Once we are successful in doing this, Avidya or ignorance vanishes.

Next comes recognising the internalities of the mind's action and its tilt or predilection to get swayed by the attractions of various luxuries.

Stop it going astray by your own mind. So, the mind is stopping the mind from going outside. This is the so-called control of the mind. We are no longer the slaves of our Indriyas and hence the slaves of our Antahkarans. The mind is killed which kills ignorance. Ignorance is killed, sorrows, fear, illusions vanish. Whatever the mind experiences, never allow it to get indulged in it. Now the intellect clearly visualises its own duties of getting retracted to the Atman. But earlier to this, it was bound by the mind's actions or the Chitta Vritti. Jivatma which has forgotten its prime duties to go to its own abode, now gets well informed by the controlled mind. So, who is now becoming the chief operator! It is our controlled, disciplined, and desireless mind. O my dear God, please do not again take me to the world and get involved in the illusion.

Hopes are to be shunned. The hopes are the real bondages. We get all sorrows because we rely on or have hopes after hopes. As we succeed in one, our hopes increase to achieve another. So, where is the end? We again rush into the whirlpool and get drowned. Hopes are to be given up entirely. Pray to God to get rid of all hopes. Only our determined mind can help us not to rest on hopes. Even if we do not get God, it hardly matters. Meeting God or realising Him solely depends on His mercy. But keeping this apart, hope not. Never shy away from performing Sadhana irrespective of results. God is the owner of all results. We are free to work. So, our mind should work without having any hopes. Peace ensues by that.

Ignorance does not touch a man of erudition. The person lacks wisdom and has ignorance, which is also termed as darkness. This world can be considered as a net of sorrows. The person of ignorance is caught by this world-net. This world-net is perplexing in nature. It is full of illusions that are transitory and are the sources of all agonies, pains, and sufferings.

IGNORANCE IS VERY POWERFUL:

Who is keeping us in illusion? It is our ignorance. Until our mind feels the need for God realisation by enquiring of the self, the ignorance binds us strongly. We get drowned by going deep and still deeper into the world of the ocean and do not find a way out. This is the great astonishment. The mind alone can control all the Indriyas. Now, let the ignorance turn towards Para-Tattva (The knowledge of the Supreme). You will observe that the ignorance vanishes and knowledge of the Atman becomes predominant.

So, now our desire to enjoy through the Indriyas has turned towards enquiring the self. The worldly desire has now turned to divine desire. This is known as redirection. Many of us wonder, how is it possible to stop the basic characteristics of greed, attachment, anger, etc.? Now the redirection works here. Our mind desires to work towards getting God. So, we are only attached towards getting the knowledge of God. But all our performances are done without any hopes and without any ownership of the various performances. And only then are we fully surrendering our powerful minds to rescue our minds from getting involved in sense pleasures and the like.

Sankalp (to get something), Vikalp (to be away from something) are not present in my mind now. I am beyond all desires. Ignorance is fully away from me. All the Chitta Vritti that I was having earlier are fully stopped. So, I have no wishes whatsoever.

My ignorance vanishes. My desires vanish. I am established in the divine self.

In the mind, we have desire. This should be treated as darkness of the night. We have conscience. This is the light of the day. Now as light expels darkness, so the conscience must destroy the desires. When the mind is completely swayed out of the worldly objects, it opens and moves about freely. It feels as if it has just got out of something which was binding it and giving them pains and sorrows. This state of the mind is indescribable. Whatever it beholds, whatever it visualises, all are nothing but the indestructible, ever-existing, and Chid Roopa (The Supreme being) Brahman. This is why we say that Brahman is Omnipresent. Apart from this whatever is imagined as the mind has no existence. You can name it as an illusion or maya. It is not only the confusion but also indicates imperfect vision. No one ever takes birth here neither dies. When the soul is a part of the Super Soul, which is constant having no beginning and no end, how come the soul is either born or dead. So, these are purely false statements. The body dies, that we agree and not the soul. If anyone who is unending, without birth or death, is the light, and is not within the ambits of the confused mind, then it is the ever-existent Atman or the Soul (Jivatma). This soul is impartial, the truth, calm, pure, unending, all-pervading, and devoid of all nuisances. In Him, the Chitta or the Manas becomes automatically pure because by the firm desire of the mind, this mind is annihilated.

MIND IS IN THE BONDAGE:

When our mind thinks that it is different from the Brahman, then only it puts itself in bondage. Exactly the opposite of this feeling, that is 'I am the Brahman,' frees the mind from all sorts of desires. When a person concentrates and thinks more about his own body and gets involved in his family affairs, he is bound. When the mind is free from various thoughts and remains beyond worldly affairs, then he is free. He never feels that he is an idol made of blood and flesh, rather by his own Antahkaran he feels completely different from this body. He is the soul and not the body. This feeling makes him free because by this feeling his ignorance is no more there. Then only these people deserve Mukti (absolute freedom). Ignorance sprouts when a person thinks all unreal as the real. Because of this ignorance, the man is bound. So, what is the solution:

ABHAYAS-VAIRAGYA, REAL AND UNREAL:

A continuous effort to elevate one's own soul (performance of Purushartha) along with extreme dispassion (This is known as Abhyas-Vairagya) is the key for a yogi. By the practice of Abhyas-Vairagya, one can become one without a second (Nirvikalpa) and gets supreme joy and happiness. My body, me all these words are the modifications of desire. This is the trick that is played by maya. So, give up all attachments of the world. Sage Rubhu says to his son, "Nidagh, O my dear son! Do not be a fool. To cry by accepting the unreal as the real is foolishness. This material body is not at all yours. This body is filled with all filthy materials like blood, flesh, and bones etc. In addition to this, this body is dumb. Why are you so much attracted to this body? And because of this body you are always thrown in the cycles of sorrowfulness and happiness by getting repeated births and deaths. It is a matter of surprise that people are bound in the nets of this body by forgetting the all-merciful Brahman. You be wise. Do all the works that form a part of your duties and never be attached to the works thus performed by you. The whole world is involved in ignorance though it has no existence. One can think it like this. Getting fibres of lotus stick a rope is made and by using this rope a large mountain is made to bind. You can well understand how inefficient this is. Can a rope made of fibres of lotus stems bind a large mountain! This is unreal. This is maya."

SWAROOP AND PARA-SWAROOP STHITI (STATE):

When we talk of the Atman, we say 'Swaroop' and when we refer to Param Atman we say 'Para-Swaroop.' Please remember, the word Para always refers to the Brahman. The Atman resides in the body, whereas Param Atman is all-pervasive.

Saint Rubhu says, "My dear son, please listen to me with due concentration." Each of the knowledge and the ignorance has 7 types of role plays. Within these 7 roles, there are numerous types of roles. Ignorance downplays the state of Swaroop. The person having ignorance is fallen and bound. Whereas establishment in the state of Swaroop is Mukti (freedom). A person having purity of the mind and proper intellect remains away from the objects of ignorance. The vices like desire, anger, greed, attachment, ego, and the likes arising out of ignorance do not pollute the Suddha (pure) state of the Swaroop. A person fully indulged in the various vices as described earlier is fully drowned in the world of the ocean. His mind finds no respite and is tethered by the poisonous snake of the mirage of the worldly pains and pleasures. There is nothing greater than these worldly attractions which perplex each human being. After going through all these attractive objects, the Jivatma makes all-out efforts to be away from these illusions. Basically, the worldly run must be over. The mind must have fully understood the bad effects of the worldly pleasures. The mind must experience the sorrows lurking in the so-called pleasures which are enjoyed by the Jivatma through the sense organs, thus avoiding the realisation of the truth and going back to its own abode. Then only, the state of Para-Swaroop will become obvious. In this state, the mind is calm, all the mind waves have vanished, the mind has become desireless, and here the mind is fully destroyed. The intellect has become non-discriminatory. It finds no difference between 'you' and 'me.' It finds no difference between the Jivatma and the Param Atma.

RAMIFICATIONS OF THE STATES (AVASTHA) OF IGNORANCE:

Vija (the seed or the start), Jagrat Avastha, Maha Jagrat Avastha, Jagrat-Swapna Avastha, Swapna Avastha, Swapna-Jagrat Avastha, and Sushupta Avastha are the 7 kinds of infatuation.

Let us discuss the characteristics of these 7 Avasthas.

In Vija Jagrat Avastha, there is no name or qualification. In this state, the Chitta is in line with pure conscience. Here, the Jivatma is known by the name and the eyes can see. This is a very new state of conscience.

Jagrat state is present behind this state. 'Me,' 'mine' feelings in the internalities sprout infatuation in this state. The feelings are created before the presence of attachment to various objects.

The Maha Jagrat Avastha reflects the inherited nature derived from the impressions of the previous birth. Here, the feelings of 'He is this,' 'I am this,' or say, this object belongs to me, etc., arise again due to the previous impression present in the mind.

Jagrat-Swapna Avastha is of 4 types. Rudha-Arudha (those which are the basics and kept in the mind without any changes). The other type is that which arises from the mental vibrations or from the Chitta Vritti. All the superimpositions arise in this state, such as seeing the brilliancy of 2 moons in one or imagining a sea shell to be silver. Here the mind is more imaginative than the real picture. You see something and superimpose something else in the vision. For example, you see a rope and imagine it to be a snake. The imagination of water in a mirage is predominant in this state. So, being in the Jagrat state, a person imagines more. The thought waves get projected and place the imagination in a different realm which is not true or say which is unreal. In this manner, the Jagrat-Swapna Avastha has many forms as there is no end to the mental waves that see reality in the unreal.

In the Swapna Avastha, what we see does not replicate as soon as we are awake. But the memory of the various scenes of the dream state remains in our mind.

Just after the Swapna Avastha, the various scenes which could not completely fructify remain in the mind during the Jagrat Avastha for a pretty long period of time. It is like a dream is seen during the awakened state. The wise call this state Jagrat-Swapna Avastha.

When the living beings overcome all these 6 states and remain like a non-living being, that state is known as Sushupta Avastha. During this state, no past feelings nor the various situations of pain and pleasure are present. In this state, the whole universe hides in utter darkness.

Thus, describing the 7 states of ignorance, Sage Rubhu now says that all the states are quite wealthy in nature. Each Avastha has numerous superimpositions of various impressions.

Now let me describe the role play of knowledge which has 7 types as well. After the knowledge of these roles of knowledge, the human being never enters the mud of ignorance.

THE RAMIFICATIONS OF KNOWLEDGE:

The wise have described quite a numerous role play of yoga. But I will describe only 7 characteristics/role plays of knowledge. Please listen. The understanding of these 7 role plays is known as knowledge. In my belief, says the sage, these 7 characteristics are meant for the welfare of human beings.

So, what is to be known (Jneya) to achieve freedom is duly described here.

The first role play is known as Subhechha (well-wish). The second one is known as Vicharana (investigation), the third is Tanu Manusi (non-attachment), the fourth is Sattwapatti (balanced state of consciousness), the fifth is Asangshakti (detached from associations), the sixth is known as Bhavna (thoughtfulness), and the seventh is known as Turyaga (a state of consciousness and non-discrimination in yoga). If in all these states there is non-existence of lamentation, then freedom can be established. Let me have a detailed discussion on these 7 roles of yoga or knowledge.

Before vairagya (dispassion) draws in the minds of a yogi, he has clearly understood the bondage (which is like a net) of the world and has duly developed mental fatigue. Rather, the human being starts enquiring about the various subject matters written in the scriptures. This state of mind is known as Subhechha.

Now comes a stage for the yogi where he has started attending to spiritual discussions made by the acclaimed saints. This is the stage when the yogi gets involved in Satsang. The yogi starts practising dispassion and forming the practices of Sadhana (Abhyasa). The wise call this Abhyasa and vairagya. As a result of this, the yogi is inclined to do pure and good work. Then we say that the Vicharana stage has duly come to the yogi. The yogi becomes investigative about the roles of the Indriyas and the other qualities of Antahkaran that were leading him to have pain and pleasure in this world.

When this state arises in the human being, they get less attached to the worldly objects. The new state that the yogi arrives in is known as the state of Tanu Manusi (non-attachment). It is a state where the mind gets detached from the world and turns to realise God.

The above 3 states, such as Subhechha, Vicharana, and Tanu Manusi states, are well practised so that they turn into regular habits of the human being. Then only by dint of strong dispassion (vairagya) purifies the mind of the yogi. As a result of this, the yogi is established in a state known as Sattwapatti. This state is a balanced state of the mind.

When the yogi has full habits of these 4 states, then he remains isolated from society in the day-to-day accomplishment of duties. This state is Asangshakti. Isolation from the hubbub of society itself is a great quality. In this state, the human mind finds time to perform spiritual Sadhana as much as possible.

These 5 states being practised, the Chitta Vritti becomes as minimal as possible and the yogi turns towards realisation of the Jivatma. The mind tends to be fully immersed in the thoughts of the soul (Jivatma). The mind is completely detached from the external and internal objects. This state is known as Bhavna or the state of thoughtfulness.

When all the above 6 states are duly practised by the yogi, the only thought that remains is getting fully involved in the enquiry of the self. The non-discriminatory power takes prominence in the minds of the yogi. He understands the pure conscience and rests his full concentration on Jivatma. This state is known as Turyaga. Here the yogi will have the qualities of Samadhan which we defined earlier. The yogis who are Jivan Mukta can have the state of Turyaga.

Note: TYPES OF MUKTI (FREEDOM):

There are 3 types of Mukti.

They are Jivan Mukta (the human being is free while the Jivatma has a body). The second type of Mukti is Videha Mukta, and the third type of Mukti is complete freedom or salvation. In this state, Soul Elevation processes are completed. The Jivatma mingles with the Param Atma or the Super Soul (Brahman/God).

The yogi, who is lucky, verily moves freely in the Jivatma. The mind is calm and peaceful. He has no anxiety. His mind does not wander aimlessly. This state is Turyaga. He remains well beyond the dualities like happiness and sorrow. A yogi who is Jivan Mukta, though involved in work, does not get attached to it. He does all obligatory duties. He never feels that he is the owner of the work accomplished by him. Because the work performed by him falls within the ambits of his duty. As a person gets up by his own friend and thereafter, he is awake, in the same way being involved in the performance of various obligatory work, his mind remains in the realm of Sanatana (That which never has a beginning nor has an end). These 7 roles of knowledge are known by the wise and the erudite. If an animal and a barbarian know about the 7 role plays of knowledge, then also they become free after their demise. When we can recognise the knots of our hearts, then we can become free. So, our prime efforts should be fully vested in the pursuance of the 7 role plays of knowledge. All the roles are to be played by the yogi to attain salvation.

AVIDYA:

Anyone who has crossed the ocean of bewilderment or infatuation will attain Param Pada (The ultimate or God). Just as the illusion of the existence of water in a mirage, thinking the unreal as real is due to the infatuation of the mind. This is precisely known as Avidya (ignorance). When the world is understood as real, when the body is considered the Jivatma, when the mind discriminates, know that all these are due to Avidya. When Avidya is destroyed, the yogi can achieve Mukti. In this state of mind, the yogi puts all his efforts into realising the Self (Atma Sakshatkar).

The process to find peace in the mind is known as yoga. It means the Chitta-Vrittis (mental vibrations) are absent. Chitta-Vrittis make the mind restless, and hence peace is lost. The yogi cannot concentrate on the real objectives. Seven role plays are described in yoga. The roles played by yoga are directed towards realising the Param Purush and achieving Brahma Pada. What is this Brahma Pada? It is the seat of the Brahman where there is no discrimination like 'myself', 'yourself', 'mine', and 'yours' and the like. At that time, you do not have to mention the name of the Lord, and there remains no emotion in the intellect. Do you know why? Because the existence of worldly objects is filled with self-emotions. There is nothing different from this. The sky is as permanent as Lord Shiva (Brahman) who is the truth; eternal; free from defects; does not require any support; causeless; indescribable; beyond Sat, Asat, and Sadasat; beginningless and has no middle; is complete and also incomplete; one cannot understand Him through mind and speech; is fully peaceful; happier than the happiest; and is obvious in Atma Sakshatkar, the Param Brahman. Brahman is never available to the yogi with emotions. So to meet Him, you should not have any sentiment or fear within yourself.

DRASTA, DARSHAN AND DRISHYA (THE TRIPLET OR TRIPUTI);

As Om is a triplet which comprises of A, U and M, in the same way, there is another triplet describing the seer, seeing and the scene. It means the seer sees the scene. So, these 3 things are involved. Here Drasta is the seer. Darshan is seeing and Drishya is the scene. In relation to the Drasta and the Drishya; the Darshan or say the Dristi, that is the interface between the 2; is fully different from the Purush in the Sakshatkar. The scene, that is created, when the Chitta travels from one city to another, we need to be fully absorbed in it always. The Sanatan Swaroop (in other words, the Brahman) is fully different from the states like Jagrat, Swapna and Sushupti. Get fully immersed in the Sanatan. It is completely different from the living and the non-living. To remain unmoved like a stone, one can resort to Tapasya or asceticism. When you give us this state, there is a void of mind. Remain in this state. The state that is created away from the Chitta is acceptable. From the principles of Param Atman, the mind is created. The world is created as an alternative to this mind. The vacuum is the creator of vacuums. From the sky, which is also a vacuum, the bluishness is manifested. When the desires vanish, at that time Chitta Vritti does not exist. As a result of this, the mist-like infatuation arising in the minds of the yogi vanishes automatically. Like the clear blue sky during autumn after the rainy season, the yogi becomes birthless and will never return to the world to have another birth. He will never fall into the cycles of birth and death henceforth. The beginning and end of all living beings are like Chinmatra (pure knowledge). Without the Seer (Drasta), sleepless dream becomes visible. This Chidatma (The ever-pure Brahman) is as pure as water, the one without a second, remains as a witness near the Jivatma, and as clear as a mirror. This Chidatma is seen as 3 different Swaroop, such as the Brahma Swaroop, the Chidakash Swaroop and Indivisible or one without a second. By thinking of the various Swaroop of Brahman, Chitta Vritti can be quelled. As we draw lines and sub-lines on any hard stone, in the same way, visualising the Omnipresent Lord is necessary. This universe is never created without the desire of the Brahman. There is the Chinmatra or the Pure Knowledge which is the Brahman. He is the creator, the maintainer, and the destroyer. So, He creates and recreates. Once this knowledge is established in the minds of human beings, they should have extreme dispassion and should have no doubts to meet the Brahman. Now the spiritual aspirant should think that he has seen what he wanted, he has known what he wanted to know. Now he has quelled his long-drawn fatigues and has taken rest.

STATE OF THE CALMNESS OF THE MIND (CHITTA):

A yogi whose mind no longer exists or is devoid of Chitta Vritti has achieved Param Pada. He has made the net of desire unsuccessful, and by doing this, he has realised Brahman. These yogis have given up their minds and become mindless. By doing this, they have increased their wisdom and erudition. Whose minds do not get attached to desires; whose Chitta-Vrittis are fully calmed; who have thoroughly studied the decisions made in the Vedantas and could make their minds duly matured by that; who are yearning for liberation and have given up all objects, useful and useless; who are regular observers or seers; never behold the world whatsoever; who are alive having decided that Para-Tattva is to be known; who have shunned the taste and the tasteless; who have become completely indifferent to the attractive transitory objects of the world and are sleeping on the path of the world that leads to utter infatuation; who have torn the nets of desires asunder due to the effects of extreme dispassion; and whose knots of the heart are duly opened; such a wise one has made themselves pure like that of the water which gets purified by the help of some pure fruits. When they have given up all bewilderment, then their mind has become free like that of a bird which is freed from a cage. At that time, the yogi becomes non-attached (Anashakta), beyond all dualities (Dwandwattita), size-less (niralamba) and free from all vices. When they have realised that God is not far, have become highly anguished with the universe which is not real, then their brilliancy becomes like that of the full Moon.

THE SEER (DRASTA):

Sat and Asat are 2 very important words described in the Vedas.

Sat: That which is the truth, or that which exists, or that which is real.

Asat: That which is false, transitory, or unreal.

I am not here and; I am not anywhere: This is the feeling of the seer. This is the true realisation of the seer. It is because Brahman is all-pervasive. So, He is here and He is also not here. In the same way, the seer must identify himself as the Brahman himself.

As without attachment, the mind is inclined towards the Drasta, the Darshan and the Drishya; in the same way, the wise perform their obligatory duties without having any attachment. Like a thief who has received an obligation from good citizens leaves thieving and gets involved in performing honest work; when a traveller suddenly enters a new village which was never conceived to be visited is taken aback with the developed roads and the developed buildings; in the same way, the wise see the luxuries in the world in utter astonishment. A controlled mind when sees the various worldly comforts, it thinks as if the comforts verily lead to pain and sufferings and due to this, the mind does not get attached to the worldly enjoyments.

MIND CONTROL METHODS:

If a king feels the comforts he derives from his kingdom have little significance when he is not attacked by enemies; the same king, if freed from a group of enemies, gets fully satisfied when he takes food from his own village. Try to have victory over the mind by massaging your own palms; by pressing your own teeth; and by creating friction of one limb against the other with force. There are no other methods left to get victory over the sea-like mind, which is full of ripples-like mental vibrations. Our internal body is like a dungeon. In the dungeon, the wicked mind is moving freely. It is very difficult to get victory over the well-decorated Indriyas by the armament-like hope. A person who has subdued the ego of his own mind; and has duly won over the Indriyas; his desire to enjoy the various worldly luxuries vanishes as lotus buds die down during pre-winter seasons. Until the mind is controlled by due concentration, the goblin-like desire never weeds out. The discerning can enslave his own mind so that whatever the intellect commands, the mind performs accordingly. As a snake is fully enslaved and works as per the directives of the snake-charmer through the recitation of certain mantras, in the same manner, the mind obeys the instructions of the intellect and hence obeys the directions of the Jivatma. This we understand that; the wise and the discerning control the mind and all the various sense organs (Indriyas). The mind fortified with reflection (manan) and meditation (dhyan) works as an affectionate woman and because it manages the Indriyas with due love, becomes a father. With the favourable knowledge of the scriptures; owing to the realisation of the self; and through the intellect; the father-like mind bestows Siddhi (perfection). The pearl-like mind, due to the shining qualities of the soul, has increased its own elegance. Now the mind becomes firm, pure, transparent, acquires the right knowledge, and is fully controlled. Due to the various impurities, it remains polluted. So, my dear son, clean the pearl-like muddy mind with water-like pure conscience. This will verily provide you brilliancy. Now engage the intellect by the support of pure conscience. By this method, all the enemies-like Indriyas will get destroyed asunder. As a result, you will cross over the ocean-like universe.

EGO AND ITS TYPES:

In this world, hope is the cause of infinite sorrows. A stateless mind is like a castle of happiness. The world appears and reappears by the bondage of desires. Desire is the bestower of pains and annihilator of all sorts of happiness. As a lion is bound in a cage, in the same way, a person who is very calm and quiet in his mind, a hero, a person from a reputable dynasty, great or highly qualified is also tethered by the net of desires. Have you seen a person who has not attained Siddhi even if he works in line with the injunctions of the scriptures and performs virtuous acts in life? I am the whole universe! I am indestructible (Achyuta)! I am Param Atman! All these statements that have complete knowledge are not treated as ego. 'I am smaller than the tip of the hair! I am beyond this illusive world!' These statements which are mixed with ego lead to salvation. These people are never bound. The persons who are in the state of Jivan Mukta have these types of ego in them.

On the other hand, he who says, 'I am this body with hands and legs and the like,' is treated to be in the lower strata of the knowledge syndrome. These people are fraught with the thoughts of the non-self and because of their ego, they form the roots of the ever-destructible tree. The lives of these people go down. These persons are far from elevating their own souls.

The wise should give up the third type of ego that produces pains and sufferings. These persons, after giving up the lower-level ego, practice Sama and achieve their welfare by the grace of God. At the outset, give up the third ego and as you rise in the higher rungs of spirituality, leave the other 2 and stay in the state of being egoless. By doing this, reaching the higher levels is possible.

MIND GETS ANNIHILATED!

Desire to enjoy any object is like inviting all sorts of sorrows. But freedom is possible when one completely gives up entertaining himself with worldly objects. The elevation of one's own mind is like the destruction of the mind itself. Annihilation of the mind happens for the lucky. The wise lose their own minds. The wise feel the mind to be neither joyful nor sorrowful. They do not perceive the mind as movable, immobile, fixed, sat, Asat, nor have the feeling that the mind is being established in any states (Avastha). But the ignorant fall into the bondage of the mind. This Chidatma is indestructible, having no name or form, and is beyond all desires. Though this pure conscience is all-pervasive, still, because of the subtlety of the sky (ether), it is not visible. This Chidatma is hundreds of times subtler than the sky and has no limbs, showing Himself as the pure universe. This Param Ataman neither rises nor sets like the Sun or the Moon. He never travels; nor is static or dynamic; never ever sits nor stands, He is neither here nor there. He never depends on others and is the one without a second. He is pure. It is the duty of the guru to encourage their disciples to practise the qualities of Sama, Dama, etc. and to make them realise, "You are like the pure Brahman." A person who has not cultivated the good qualities as described in the scriptures, if you tell them, 'You are like pure Brahman', then these words never make them understand the truth, and it is like pushing such unwise individuals into the dungeon. We need to give the knowledge of the Vedantas to those whose Antahkaran has become pure because of wisdom and who have given up the desires of the various pleasures of the world. This world exists because of the pure conscious Chidatma, as light is seen through candles, as day shines on the rising of the Sun, and as the flower spreads fragrance when it blooms. Speaking practically, the world is like the fragrance of the flower or the brilliance given out by the sunshine. The world exists because of the Chidatma. When a person is fully established in the pure conscience or the Chidatma, the world is fully destroyed for them. When the veil of ignorance is uncovered from you and you have the brilliance of the Chidatma, at that time you will be established in your own Swaroop.

Here Saint Rubhu emphasises that at such a stage, you can really feel the essence of my advice.

When the best Avidya is all-out to destroy the selfishness; by that, the wisdom, which is the annihilator of all bad qualities, is obtained by the native. As a sword can work against another sword and eventually destroys it; in the same manner, an enemy verily destroys another enemy like that of a poison destroys some other poison. As a result, the illusion gets satisfied by the destruction of the Avidya. Its Swaroop is not seen as such. At that time, all the illusions vanish, and the truth becomes prominent. This illusion is verily not there, and the Brahman is having its existence leads to freedom. At this stage, there is no discrimination which leads to achieving the ultimate.

FORMS OF JIVATMA:

O my dear son, says Rubhu, what does not happen is known as the bestower of the indestructible. You need not brood over the creation of this illusion or maya. You need to think of the ways and means so that it will be possible on your part to destroy this maya. When the process becomes conspicuous, then only one can think of achieving the position of the indestructible (Akshay Pada-Prapti). From where this illusion sprouts, and what is its true nature and how this can be destroyed, should be thought of so that the root cause of this disease can be completely eradicated. If you can uproot this evil in yourself, then you will not fall into the repeated cycles of birth and death, and you will illumine yourself as the pure consciousness eventually. First, one should have a conviction that this Chitrupa is a part of the Brahman. It is as pure as the Brahman itself. This Chit Shakti is little aggrieved with the ocean-like Param Atman. The pure Chit is rising like the ripples in the ocean. As the air has ripples in the sky, in the same way, the Jivatma also jumps as ripples in the ocean-like Param Atman. The cause of the accomplishment of the whole gets into these temporary ripples. This is the Atma Shakti and it is established in the Param Atman which has the highest level. The worldly limitations and the activities thereof are quite incapable of driving the powers of Jivatma. Because of this Chit Shakti is not obvious due to its limitations and thus it has the thought of a shape. When this thought of the shape becomes predominant, at that time it has a name and number. This Chit Shakti enters definite boundaries and does various activities. Because of these activities, it takes into alternate forms and is termed as Kshetrajna (knower of the field or the body). The body is the field. Then he becomes the owner of the ego basis the imagination of the various desires. The definite and polluted ego is known as intellect. When this intellect takes the shape of desires, at that time it becomes the mind. When the mind slowly enters the realm of dualities with strong to stronger determination, it takes the form of the Indriyas. The wise name the body with the hands and legs to be the Indriyas. In this manner being bound by the desire and temptation, the living being having drawn into the ropes of sorrows, goes down and down. As a silkworm gets into the nets of the cocoon duly made by it, in the same way, the powerful Chit also enters the nets of the world due to its own ego. The lion-like Chit Shakti being fallen in its own net becomes very discouraged and dispirited. This Atman is known as the Chit somewhere and in some other place, it is named as the ego. This Atma is named as the intellect somewhere; and is termed as mind in a different perspective; and in some other spheres, it is known as wisdom. He is termed as the owner of all the activities, and based on situations is also known as the mind, and in some other references, this Atman is known as nature. The human body has 8 constituent parts. These 8 parts together are known as Puryastaka. In some situations, the Jivatma is termed as Puryastaka and in other situations, this is termed as the bondage. This Atman is the wish in some places and it becomes Avidya in some other situations. The Brahman is the creator of this fruitless banyan tree and He holds the Jivatma present in all types of bodies like the seed of this banyan tree.

CREATION OF THE INDRIYAS:

As an elephant slips into mud, in the same way, this mind is burnt by the fire of thoughts; is cut by the python of anger; and is drowned by the whirlpool of the sea of lust and temptation. This mind has forgotten its own grandfather, the Jivatma. Hence, you should rescue this mind as your first duty. Numerous minds being supported by the Jivatma and due to the imagination of the Param Atman are created and duly nurtured. As in the streams, the water molecules are created and remain there, in the same way, the various minds and their feelings are also created and remain like that in the future by the Jivatma. Some of the vibrations of the minds are created many a time; and yet some others are created only for 2 times or 3 times and are remaining as they are. There are some vibrations which are created only once. All these have names and forms. Some are named in the forms as Sun, Moon, Hari, Shiva, Varun, Brahma etc. Some others are named and having forms as Kinnar, Yaksh, Gandharv and naga etc. Some are named as Brahman, Kshatriya, Vaishya, Shudra etc. Some are named in the form of trees such as palm, tamal, kadam, lemon, mango, grass, medicinal plants, roots, leaves, and fruits. Some others have become quite static like the mountains such as Meru, Malay, Mahendra et al. Some have the forms of water, seas, oceans, milk, clarified butter, sugarcane juice etc. Many of the Bhavas take the shape of various directions like east, west, north and the south. Some are present in the forms of very speedy rivers. Some have taken the shapes of various materials such as balls, tops which are made up and down repeatedly. There are many which rise high and some others fall from high altitudes. There are many human beings who have wisdom and have the right conscience. But they do not do good work. For these people their repeated births and deaths do not end. When the Atma Tattva by the effects of places and times and by the influences of its own powers takes the shape of any entity, at that time it is running towards the minds with the attractions of the various desires and temptations. Getting fully engrossed in the so-called temptations and desires, the Mana Shakti (power of the mind) gets indulged in the clear sky within a moment and sprouts as the sound-like seed. Further, this mind duly concentrated and indulged by the vibrations of the air, is travelling as vibrations of air. In this air, the touch becomes the seed. Again, this mind by dint of its unrelenting practices creates sky (Akash) consisting of sound-touch (Sabda-Sparsa). This Akash collides with Vayu (air) and creates Fire (Agni). This Agni in cooperation with the Tanmatra (Mana, Buddhi, Ahamkara and Chitta), transforms to Triguna (3 qualities: Sattva, Rajas, Tamas). We have discussed about Triguna earlier. Now the mind in association with the Triguna creates the feelings of various tastes (Gandha). At that time this mind thinks of the coldness of water and contemplates about water. Now these Triguna along with the taste, thinks and feels of Kshiti (Earth). In this manner, the Pancha Tanmatra (Kshiti, Aap, Tej, Marut and Vyom) which are the 5 basic elements (Pancha Bhuta) join and they leave their subtlety so that they can visualise the body being in the Akash in the form of sparks of fire. This body is having the characteristics of ego and joined with the intellect as the seed. This way this body is known as Puryastaka (the 8 constituents). All these Tanmatra are placed in the lotus of the heart as a black-bee (The heart is construed as lotus. It is termed as Hrida-Padma in Sanskrit).

THE RIGHT STRATEGY TO CROSS THE WORLD OF OCEAN:

As a mature Bilwa fruit turns hard, in the same way, the subtle body (Sukshma Sharira) thinks firmly about a brilliant body. And due to this thought, only the Sthula Sharira (gross body) is created. This brilliancy of the body is like the gold on the body of a mouse seen in a clear sky and takes the shape as per its own characteristics. This body becomes like a head on the top; like the hands on the sides; like the legs on the lower side; and like the stomach in the middle. This way it converts itself into a complete body. This body, accomplished by the intellect, strength, semen, inspiration, conscience, and wealth, becomes Pitamah Brahma of all the Lokas. (Trilokas: Bhuh, Bhuvah and Swah & Saptaloka: Bhuh, Bhuvah, Swah, Mahah, Janah, Tapah and Satyam).

Brahma Ji has become obvious in this manner. He is the knower of the past, the present and the future. He has a very handsome body. He looked at the subtle sky and could not find any beginning point nor the end point of this. So, what is the beginning here! Thinking this, he got his own consciousness and could remember the various events of his previous creation (Brahmaji the creator. This work is assigned to him by the Brahman). He could now remember the equality of all religions. By his own desire, he started creating many colours and shapes. He also started creating many subjects meant for different territories. He also started creating different types with picturesque objects, underlined various procedures, created various scriptures, and imagined heaven-hell etc., so that living beings can achieve Dharma, Artha, Kama and finally Moksh. My dear son, this mind is like the Brahman. Because, due to its power of imagination, the whole universe along with Brahma Ji exists. When the lifespan of Brahma Ji ends, at that time the mind also disappears. Oh Brahman, my son! In this universe no one is born nor dies. Whatever is visible is illusion or false. This world is like the scales of the hoax-like snake. It is best to give up this world. The city where the angels live, whether it is well-organised or kept unorganised, matters little. Because these have very little significance. They are all maya. There is no truth there. So why should we obey what is happiness or sorrowfulness. All the relatives including the wives, the progeny and the wealth are like hoaxes. They do not exist. When attachment and illusion grow, no one ever gets happiness. No one has satisfaction nor peace. For the objects which are dear to the ignorant are not at all liked by the wise. All such objects seen are like burdens for the wise because they do not derive any pleasure from all such objects. So, O my dear son! Be wise. Have knowledge of the Brahman. Do not run after worldly enjoyments and worldly objects. These are not the truth. Never desire what is not yours and try your best to enjoy what belongs to you. This is wisdom. This is knowledge. This verily elevates. This provides peace and you be the controller of your mind and not vice versa. So, we should not accept what is not the truth. We have seen the water on a lotus leaf. The lotus leaf is not attached to the water, though it has water on top of it. In the same manner, work by being rightly resolved, but do not get attached to the work. Peace immediately ensues by performing all duties this way. Here our intellect does not get involved. It is free from all sorts of attachments. If your heart does not beat by seeing a worldly object, then you have already acquired knowledge about the various worldly objects that are to be known. Hence, after acquiring knowledge of the world and being indifferent to worldly pleasure, entertainment, joy and whatsoever; you can cross over the worldly ocean. When after receiving the nice smell of the flower, you do not attach your mind there, then it is possible that you achieve the higher levels.

MIND IS TO BE PURIFIED:

The world of ocean is filled with water which is like desires. A wise person who has placed himself on the knowledge of a boat or ship has crossed this ocean. So, what is very important is wisdom or Jnana. A person who has understood this illusive world will never get perturbed by the weird behaviour of the various entities at large and will never leave them. Rather than being in the world, he verily remains unattached to the illusive objects, entities, relatives, friends, wealth, and whatsoever seems attractive to his own mind. He rather gets attached to understanding and being in Atma Tattva as soon as various desires sprout. Look, this is a great redirection! All the desires for the world are redirected to be in the Atma Tattva and not attached to the worldly objects, being in the world. It is because the determination becomes more and more firm. Eventually, the Chittakash ceases to be dynamic. Its vibrations do not happen. It means the person has no Chitta Vritti or no mental vibrations. As a seed slowly grows into a seedling and then into a plant; in the same way, the conscience understanding itself as not to be the Self remains attached to the desires. With the growth of the desires, the activities appear. And very quickly these activities proliferate very quickly. But these activities do not bestow happiness. Rather, the person gets pains and sufferings. And hence, my dear son, resist the activities that enhance desires in the mind. In the case of the appearance of desires, never give way to the thoughts of worldly objects. It is because any decisive and firm efforts to refute the desires to take prominence will not allow the various activities to happen. If thoughts are quelled, desires die down on their own. Win the mind by the mind and spoil the desires by the desires. This way, by being in the Self, become a positive and industrious human being. Work towards the realisation of the soul as your own sole objective. The world is just a vacuum like that of the Akash. There are 3 doshas (obstacles) in a human being. They are known as Mala, Vikshepa, and Avarana.

Mala: The impurities of the mind. These are removed by doing the right work (karma yoga).

Vikshepa: This is the outward tendency of the mind. This obstacle is removed by meditation (Dhyana yoga).

Avarana: The curtain of ignorance. This is removed by the practices of Jnana Yoga.

As we remove the dirt (copper oxide) from copper and husk from paddy; in the same way, by doing the right work, we can remove the impurities of our minds.

THE STATE OF SAMADHI:

Sage Rubhu addressing his son as sinless, says, "Move in this world by keeping aside the internal hopes and by giving up feelings like wealth. Think that you are not the owner. If you do like this, you will have impartiality as your own characteristic which is like elixir for you. Happiness and sorrowfulness are created by human beings. If you understand this well, then you have equality as your balanced character. Once you have fully accepted the quality of being impartial and equal, the basic cause of your various movements will cease. Leave the duties and the non-performances, and drink your mind (When the mind has no existence); in such a state, be established in Samadhi. The pure conscience will take the shape of desire in the mind. This way the roots of basic desire will get annihilated and your internalities become as pure as the sky, you will get peace in your mind. When all the desires disappear from the heart of hearts, you will be free and will never have anxiety in your mind. When the mind is under illusion, it moves in all 10 directions (The 10 directions are east, west, north, south, north-east, north-west, south-east, south-west, up, and down) so that it sees what is to be seen. Jivatma is present all over this body (internal-external, up-down); and for him, the world does not become unreal. However, the persons become wise, being involved in the undeterred performance of virtuous work. These people deserve to cross the ocean-like world."

SUBDUING THE SENSE ORGANS (INDRIYAS):

I am different, they are different; these feelings lead to illusion. We should give up these feelings so that equality is prevalent. It is not a place where I do not exist. There is a scarcity of Atman in the various objects. As a matter of fact, all these are Sat (eternal) and Chinmaya (Supreme Consciousness). All these are verily the 'Brahman.' In this state of mind of equality and impartiality, Shoka (lamentation), Moha (attachment), old age, and birth do not exist. There is not a possibility of an iota of imagination so far as Sat-Chit-Anand (Truth-Consciousness-bliss) Parameswara (God) is considered. Everything exists in the Atma Tattva (Knowledge of the Self). This is why anything that is easily available enjoy without attachment and never think of any more objects. Neither give up nor accept anything. In this way be beyond all confusions. For a person whose present human birth is the end and who is subject to non-return to the world; wisdom enters in him, like the best valuable pearl. We can say by our own experience that the happiness obtained by a person having strong dispassion in seeing God is out of his positive vibes of Atma Tattva, and we pray to Him properly. We pray to the Atman, who is in between the truth and the illusive world. This Atman is the light of all lights and is seated in our body like Lord Maheswara. Persons who take care of worldly objects by giving up the eternal Atman give up their own Kaustubh Mani (a valuable jewel of the sea) and want to have other jewels (worldly objects are referred to as inferior jewels) which are inferior having little value. All the Indriyas, may be strong or weak, deserve thrashing by the stick of our own conscience. As Indra assaults the large mountains with his thunderbolt (it is known as Vajra: mythological terminology of a very powerful weapon), in the same way, we need to subdue the Indriyas (sense organs) by our intelligence and conscience.

This body is like this elusive world. We can compare this body with the dreaded dreams that we see in the dream state (Swapna Avastha). It has an impure spread. This body has ignorance during childhood. During the young period, the body is killed by the attractive arrows of the eyes of the spouse. And hence during the last stage, what benefits can be available from the spouse and children! Asat is situated over Sat; ugly is situated over the gorgeous, and sorrowfulness is situated over truthfulness. Knowing all these, to whom should I surrender? The Brahman or Purush has covered the beginning and end of the universe in a flick and within the shortest twinkling of His eyes. When this Purush is subject to time, in such a universe, where is my position? I am a mere human being. How this body, which is bound within the perimeters of this sorrowful world, can taste the essence of this body. My impure mind is the thief who is stealing this Atman. I did not know when my Atman was stolen by my mind. But now I have known about this thief. I will annihilate my mind. There is no benefit in feeling sorry for the unacceptable, vile objects. At the same time, getting attached to the useful objects is also wasteful. So, let me be established beyond the objects that are useful or vile. It is because a wise has the following qualities, such as eternity, awareness, equality, non-activity, desirelessness, depression with the illusive world, uniqueness, gracefulness, softness, fortitude, amity, peacefulness, and ability to speak sweetly etc. Here desire is the hunter. It has spread the net of temptation. You are bound by this net. All thoughts are like threads. You are thinking that there is water in the mirage of hopes. This mirage is spread all around. Cut this net by the sword-like knowledge and stand aloft like that of the cyclone which cut the nets of the clouds.

CUT THOSE DESIRES ASUNDER;

The helve of an axe is made of wood. This axe is capable of cutting trees. Exactly in the same argument, annihilate your mind with your mind and establish yourself in the purest level. Think that getting up and sitting down; standing and walking; sleeping and awakening etc. states of a human being do not have any significance. By having such affirmations, withdraw your concentration from these scenes. Because, the Chitta verily becomes tethered when it gets involved in the various scenes. Do not bother, who is standing or sitting or doing some work or is sleeping. All these states are not our objectives. As soon as you give up these worldly scenes, you will be fit to achieve freedom. Be as firm as a mountain with the feeling that 'this world does not exist;' 'I do not exist.' Know that the Drasta (seer) is the Jivatma and the scenes are the Drishya. Now you are the Darshan (the intermediary). This is to be clearly convinced by you and by yourself. Understand that the 'charm' is the scene, the owner of the 'charm' is the Jivatma. Now you being the intermediary, meditate on this 'charm' and be one with the Param Atman. Do remember one useful statement, "The living being is freed being fastened by a rope; but it is not getting freedom from the bondage being in the worldly desires." Knowing this to be certain, cut the desires asunder. If you want to know the reason, please understand the desires are combined with ego and these are having the resolve to be in this illusive world. And know that the egoless mind is the sharp sword to kill all the desires in you. Birth and death are horrible. The living beings are there. Now you should move without fear in the realm of the Paramarth (God). Anything absolves us from the desires and bestows us peace of mind, is to be pursued with sincerity. How you can establish yourself in the state of the Param Atman who has no beginning and no end, is by thinking strongly that, 'these things do not belong to me' and 'I have no ownership of all these worldly objects.'

'ME' AND 'MINE': THE LOWER NATURE:

Our intellect does not have the lower thoughts of 'me' and 'mine' when equality is predominant. By having these feelings, living beings give up the bondage of this body. So what becomes our prime duty is giving up all sorts of temptations and attachments. We call those as Jivan Mukta who give up the desires fraught with ego and leave the objectives to be meditated upon. These people are free. When we completely uproot our own resolves to have desires, then only peace ensues. A Jivan Mukta is quite capable of sacrificing these resolves. These yogis or these Purushas are the best among the knowers of the Brahman. The yogis, being freed from all worries, achieve the Param Brahman. The yogis have the qualities of Sama and Dama and the rest of the qualities. Due to these reasons, they never get involved in the happiness and sorrowfulness of this world. They are free from all those they wish and are free from all those they do not wish. The yogis who behave as if they are in a slumber get the true freedom from this world. A desireless person does not care for Kama (attachment/lust), Krodha (anger), Moha (delusion), Harsha (happiness), Amarsha (sorrowfulness), and Bhaya (fear) and never be the slaves of all these vices. They never have the sense of pleasure or pain. They are established beyond all the vibrations of the mind. When the interest and strong desire to get something are not resident in the minds of the yogis, they get peace and tranquillity. They have equanimity and are established in the Param Pada. The yogis know that an iota of desire is also quite capable of giving way to bondage. The yogis give up all the objects that are either Sat or Asat and get established at the highest level. To believe in freedom or to believe in bondage, to believe in the Sat and to believe in Asat; all these beliefs are the root causes of happiness and sorrowfulness. Give up all these and remain as peaceful as that of the calm water of the Pacific Ocean.

FOUR AFFIRMATIONS OF A HUMAN BEING;

A man has 4 affirmations.

1. My body is created by my parents. This is the first affirmation.

2. I am a soul (Atman), subtler than the subtlest tip of a hair. This should be the second affirmation. Because of this affirmation, the sages achieve final emancipation.

3. Based on all matters of this universe, I am the all-pervading Atman without a beginning and an end. This affirmation is the cause of salvation.

4. I and this whole universe are nothing but a vacuum like the Akash. This fourth affirmation verily bestows Mukti.

The first affirmation is the cause of bondage as it pertains to the body.

The other 3 affirmations have pure and immaculate desires. The persons who have these 3 affirmations are involved in Atma Tattva and are in Jivan Mukta states.

The people who think that everything belongs to the soul never fall into the whirlpool of sorrows time and again.

STATE OF BEING PURE:

The vacuum that is called the Jivatma is the illusion (maya) of nature, the Shiva, Purush, Ishan, the Truth, and is Brahma Jnana. The dual and the dual energy related to the Param Brahman visualised as the dual. The person who remains away from this unreal world and is established in solipsism (thinking himself as the pure soul) is beyond satisfaction-dissatisfaction. These people have supreme knowledge (Chinmaya) and never fall in this poisonous world. So, "O my dear son! Knowing this, remain in the state of desireless having no attachment to the world. This way you remain without worldly sufferings, and your stay in this world is quite casual. Though you show anger outside, your internalities are ruled by calmness and serenity. Show to the outside that you are the owner of all activities performed by you; but leave ownership of everything. Always think internally that you are not the doer. Maintain yourself like a person of pure and divine Antahkaran. In this state move across the Bhuh Loka. If a person rates the enemies and the friends equally; performs his own obligatory duties being free from desires and non-desires; who has neither predilection nor attraction towards the various worldly objects; is sweet-spoken and comprehends the basis of all other entities; has no lamentation nor sorrowfulness. Such a person is quite indifferent to pain and pleasure. So, my dear son, giving up ego, remain aloof from all sorts of impure activities. As the Akash is clear being a vacuum, you must lead yourself exactly like that in this world."

DETACHMENT: DESIRELESSNESS:

All your activities must be noble and pure. You must follow the principles of high standards of living. You should remain unperturbed while dealing with various situations. Your mind does not hanker after the achievement of worldly objects. Your internalities are guided by extreme dispassion. People of low intellect have attitudes like, 'he is my friend or he is my enemy.' For them, the whole world is considered as one family only. You need to be beyond all existences and non-existences, beyond the considerations of old age and death. Establish yourself in a position where all divine desires are supported by your pure intellect. This is the state of desirelessness. Also, we call that such a person has the state of Brahman. The Sadhaka whose state is like this remains away from infatuation in dangerous situations. Elevation of the mind is eventually achieved by studying and abiding by the injunctions of the scriptures, and by performing activities that are fortified with dispassion. If a person is under the control of hopelessness, he cannot accomplish the basic benefits of vairagya (dispassion) whatsoever. If the minds of the Sadhakas are indulged in various hopes, then he becomes fully passionate like that of the water in a pond during autumn. It is not understood why a person having a dispassionate mind is not ashamed of giving way to passion, attachment, anger, and the likes? Bondage ensues when the mind and the enjoyment of illusive objects are firmly united together. Freedom from bondage is known as Mukti. Vedantas declare that freedom from Chitta Vritti which is inclined towards the world is the Atman. See yourself through Antahkarans by realising and accepting this truth. By doing this, one will be seated in the state of being blissful. This Bhuh layer, the various directions (east, West etc.) and the Jivatma; all are this, Chit. I am Chit. This Chit (ever-pure, clean, and clear) which is manifested has no brilliancy. It has turned into Drasta having witnessed the Drishya and Darshan. I am merely the great conscience. I am complete, filled with radiance, free from empathy, always free and Chid Roopa (wise and intelligent). Now Sage Rubhu concludes by saying to his son that he should pacify all mental vibrations and give up all desires entirely.

This spiritual discussion between Saint Rubhu and his son Nidagh sheds spiritual light on all of us. We are supposed to follow his advice to be free.

OM (PRANAB) SADHANA:

We have talked about 3 states (Avastha). Awaken, Dream, and slumber (Jagrat, Swapna, and Sushupti) are the 3 states. The other 2 states are Turiya and Turiyattita.

Let us discuss achieving the Turiya Avastha through OM Sadhana. We need to understand that all these 5 states are states of consciousness.

Turiya is a state of transcendental consciousness. Here, the focus is both inward and outward simultaneously. Here, the yogi remains beyond love, thoughts, will, sentiments, etc. It is difficult to describe this state. It is a state of incomprehensibility.

Turiyattita is the ultimate state of consciousness. It is filled with bliss. The yogi becomes Jivan Mukta in this state.

Through OM Sadhana, we can reach the Turiya State. However, it does not lead to complete freedom.

As we have already stated, OM has 3 constituents: A, U, and M. If we treat Pranab or OM as a divine swan, then its right wing is 'A', the left wing is 'U', the tail is 'M', and the point (known as Ardha Matra) is the head.

The 3 qualities are Sattva, Rajas, and Tamas. The body of this divine swan is known as Sattva. Its 2 legs are Rajas and Tamas. Dharma (what should be done) is the right eye, and adharma (what should not be done) is the left eye.

We already know that the Sapta (7) Loka consists of Bhuh, Bhuvah, Swah, Maha, Janah, Tapah and Satyam. How do we attribute these Lokas to the various body parts of the divine swan! Its navel is attributed to Maha Loka. Its waist is the Swaha Loka. The thighs are the places of Bhuvah Loka and its feet are attributed to Bhuh Loka. The heart of the divine swan is attributed to Janah Loka, Tapah Loka is in the throat. Satyam Loka is attributed to the frontal part of the head and is also attributed to the eyebrows part of the divine swan.

This divine swan is treated as the Pranab Swaroop. The Sadhaka rides on this swan and institutes Pranab Sadhana along with due meditation. The spiritual aspirant does reflective thinking (Manan-Chintan) on Pranab (OM). By doing this, he becomes absolved from thousands of sins that were committed by him in the past. Such a spiritual performance leads the Sadhaka to attain ultimate freedom.

'A' is the Agni demigod of OM. Its Swaroop is like Agni Mandala (The realm of fire). Its first syllable (Matra) is 'Agneyee'.

The second syllable is 'U.' Its demigod is Vayu. Its Swaroop is like Vayu Mandala (The realm of air). The second syllable is known as Vayabya.

The third syllable is 'M.' Its Swaroop is Surya (The demigod Sun). Its Swaroop is like Surya Mandala. The fourth half-syllable (Ardha Matra) is Chandra Bindu. Its deity is Varuna.

All the 3 and a half Matras have 3 beautiful heads. This is why Pranab is versed in 12 qualities (Dwadas Kalatmaka).

In Ashtanga Yoga (Eight limbs of Yoga) written by Maharshi Patanjali, the combination of Dharana (Concentration of the mind on a particular object), Dhyana (Sustained concentration of the mind on that object) and Samadhi (Getting deeply absorbed in the inner essence of that object) is known as Samyam. From here on, we will use the term Samyam for the combination of Dharana, Dhyana and Samadhi.

The one and only benign way to know this Dwadas Kalatmaka Pranab is through Samyama.

Now let us understand how the 12 Matras of Pranab are named.

The first matra is named 'Ghoshini', the second 'Vidyut', the third 'Patangini', the fourth 'Vayu Begini', the fifth 'Naamadhaya', the sixth 'Aindri', the seventh 'Vaishnavi', the eighth 'Shankari', the ninth 'Mahati', the tenth 'Dhriti', the eleventh 'Mouni', and the twelfth matra is known as 'Brahmi'.

If the aspirant leaves the body being in the first matra, then he takes the new body as the 'monarch of the world.' If he leaves the body being in the second matra, then in the next birth he takes the body of a 'famous Yaksh.' Likewise, in the third matra, the new body becomes 'Vidyadhar,' in the fourth, the body becomes 'Gandharv', in the fifth, it is 'Ushita' and lives in the Chandra Loka. In the sixth after death, the aspirant gets the close union (Sajujya) with Lord Indra. In the seventh matra, the new body gets the feet of Lord Vishnu. In the eighth matra, the new body gets near Lord Shankara. If the body departs in the ninth matra, the aspirant resides in the Maha Loka. In the tenth matra, the new place for the aspirant is in 'Dhruva Loka.' In the eleventh matra, the Sadhaka resides in Tapa Loka. If the body leaves in the twelfth matra, then the Sadhaka gets Brahma Loka. This way, there is upliftment of the Sadhaka. It is needed that the Sadhaka should perform Purushartha of the Pranab in such a manner that he gets the Brahma Loka.

To know the Param Brahman, there is still another way which is adjudged to be higher, the best, pure, and prosperous means than that of the previous ones. By adhering to this methodology, the Sadhaka will come across various brilliant splendours such as the brilliance of the fire, the Sun, and the Moon.

When the mind and the Indriyas of the Sadhaka remain beyond the 3 qualities such as Sattva, Rajas, and Tamas, and get fully absorbed in the essence of the Param Brahman (Sadashiva who is beyond all qualities) being in peace; such a state is known as 'The state of Yoga.'

Thus, the Sadhaka who traces the path of yoga with complete devotion and attachment to God should leave all the worldly attractions and strive to give up 'ego' slowly. Now the yogi, after leaving the above vices, attains full isolation from the world and verily becomes one with the Param Atman.

All the wise should put their efforts into knowing the soul and its Swaroop always. It is also advised for everyone to mentally remember God most of their valuable time. We have performed some good and some bad work (karma) in our past lives. Those karmas that remained as a carry forward to the present life are known as Prarabdha. In the present life, we must enjoy all the balance karmas owing to Prarabdha (however painful or hardships they bestow) without any hesitation. The reason is, "Even if a Sadhaka visualises the soul, still the Prarabdha does not vanish. All the Karmas remain. Even in this life, we may not enjoy all the Prarabdha karmas. In such cases, the karmas get carried over to another birth. So be careful and do not ignore Prarabdha." In a dream, all that we see remains as it is until we are dreaming. As soon as we wake up, the scenes during our dream seem to be untrue. In the same way, as soon as the Sadhaka experiences and fully understands Tattva Jnana, all karmas owing to Prarabdha vanish as visualised by the wise and the erudite.

The accomplished yogi does not have a new birth. Hence, for these yogis, Prarabdha is not relevant. Exactly in the same way, during the dream state, knowledge of the body and the rest never becomes obvious. These persons do not have any impressions of their bodies during the dream state. But, in the awakening state, we have the impression of our own bodies.

When a person has the impressions of some objects, they can understand from where these objects have come. But for objects that have no impressions, a person cannot tell about the origin and the state of the object. As soil is the cause of an earthen pot, similarly, the soul is the cause of this illusive body.

As per the Vedantas, the impressions of the illusive worldly objects are due to ignorance. When ignorance vanishes and knowledge prevails, various affairs of this world disappear. There is a saying, "Rajju Bhujangam Pratibhasita Vai." It means when a person sees a rope, he gets frightened thinking the rope is a snake. This illusion is because of ignorance. In this logic, we infer that the ignorant, without the knowledge of the soul, think the world is the truth or is real.

When the person clearly understands and recognises the rope properly, the thought that 'it is a snake' vanishes. In the same way, when we realise our own souls, the earlier thought that 'the world is real' no longer holds.

This body is also not real. So, the existence of the body does not arise. In this way, when a Sadhaka reaches this state, Prarabdha vanishes.

Prarabdha is told for the ignorant. This Prarabdha has no significance for a God-realised person. We have known that after clouds uncover the Sun, we can see the sunrise. Similarly, when the soul and the Brahman are thought by a Sadhaka as one due to the disappearance of Prarabdha, he meets with the param Atman in the form of a sound (Nada).

What should the yogi do? First, the yogi should sit in Siddhasana and then perform Vaishnavi Mudra. Staying in this mudra, listen to the nada in the right ear. As the yogi advances in listening to the nada, the outside sounds are duly covered. It means that the yogi does not listen to the outside sounds while listening to the nada in the right ear with deep concentration. In this manner, as the yogi advances, he wins over the 'A' and 'M' matra, which are the 2 wings. Further advancement of the yogi listening to the nada for a long period of time, the yogi wins over Pranab or OM. By performing this Pranab Sadhana, the yogi achieves the Sun, i.e. accomplishes Atma Sakshatkar.

As the yogi listens to the nada, it takes various forms. And not only that, but the intensity of the nada also rises. The yogi listens to the nada loudly. But as this period of the practice increases, the nada becomes smoother and smoother progressively.

In the beginning, the sound as listened to by the yogi is in the forms of sounds of clouds, of streams, and of trumpets. Intermittently, the yogi listens to the nada in the forms of the sounds of drum, of clarion, and of bells. Towards the end, the nada is listened to by the yogi in the melody forms of the sounds of honey bees, of violin, of flute, and of ornaments worn on the feet by ladies.

These sounds, which are listened to by the yogi, become smooth and smoother from loud and louder as the time of the practices increases. The Sadhaka should transition from loud to smooth nada and vice versa. During these alternate transitions, the yogi is advised not to think about any other things. His mind should only listen to the nada. The characteristic of the mind is to be attracted to one sound and finally get absorbed in the same sound as the time elapses.

When the mind forgets all the illusions of the world, like that of the water when mixed with milk, it becomes one with the Chidakash of the nada. Now the disciplined person should listen to the sound that he likes most. This is because the mind is fully engrossed in the nada. The listener should forget all the thoughts and seek the nada of his choice. As a honeybee does not bother about the existence of the flower while tasting its honey, in the same way, the mind while listening to the nada of its choice verily forgets the odour that is present in the various worldly desires. As a snake is charmed and becomes elated while listening to melodious music, in the same way, our minds also get charmed and elated by listening to the nada. By doing this, the mind forgets about its fickleness. If the mind forgets about the worldly fickleness, then its concentration augments and it ceases to be wandering hither and thither. Our mind can be compared to an elephant which is rambling because it has worldly desires. As a sharp anlius (ankush) is used by the mahout to control the elephant, similarly, the mind is controlled by listening to the nada of its own choice.

Let us say we compare the mind to a deer and the waves of a river. Just as a deer is goaded by melodious music and caught in a net; just as the banks of a river resist its waves; similarly, nada can stop Chitta Vritti or the vibrations of the mind.

When the mind is engrossed with the nada, it has started feeling the existence of Param Atman. The mind exists until the existence of nada. When nada becomes weak and weaker, the state of mindfulness becomes the opposite. The nada becomes fully merged in the Akshar Brahma (OM), but its memory remains in the mind of the yogi. When there is no sound in the nada, then we can understand that it is Param Pada. When the yogi seeks after the nada and could come across a situation when the desires are fully vanished, then we can understand that his mind and the breath are merged in the Param Atman. So, we can say that thousands of nada and thousands of Bindu are merged in Pranab.

When a yogi is beyond the Avastha-Tray (Awake, Dream, and slumber) and resembles as dead by leaving all the worldly desires and the thoughts thereof, he is established in Mukta-Avastha undoubtedly. These yogis, after reaching this state, never listen to any sounds such as the sound of a drum or that of the sound of a conch.

When the mind has no thoughts, it becomes like dry wood in the body. It loses its sensitivity. All dualities like hot-cold, happy-sad, etc., become irrelevant for the yogi. He does not find any difference between praise and disparage. The yogi is thus established in the state of Samadhi, leaving all these feelings. The fixity of his mind overpowers the requirement of Jagrat, Swapna, and Sushupti Avasthas. Leaving Jagrat and the Swapna states, the yogi establishes himself in his own Swaroop. His vision becomes fixed, the breath becomes immobile without any efforts, the Chitta Vritti are quelled. The yogi is said to be in the Turiya state. This state is beyond Jagrat, Swapna, and Sushupti.

TURIYATTITA AVASTHA:

Unless the Turiyattita Avastha is attained by the yogi, merging with the Lord is not possible. The Pranab Sadhana, which was just described with its characteristics and actions, brings the yogi very near to attaining the highest level. So, let us discuss this state.

This state is described through a dialogue between Lord Narayan (The Brahman) and Lord Brahma (Brahma is created by Lord Narayan).

Brahma was asking Lord Narayan to explain the path traced by the Avadhutas (These saints are rare and they have attained the highest siddhis by virtue of their strong and innate Spiritual Sadhana), who have attained the state of Turiyattita. He also wanted to know from the Lord what the basic states of the Avadhutas are.

Lord Narayan replies: "Saints who walk in the spiritual path of Avadhutas are rare. There are very few Avadhutas available in the world. They are eternal, ideals of complete renunciation, sources of all knowledge, respected by all and are known as Veda Purush. Such great saints keep me in their minds and I reside in their internalities. They surpass the levels of monks starting with Kutichaka, then Bahudaka, then Hamsa and finally surpass the levels of Param Hansa."

==

Note: Actually, there are various stages of renunciation. It starts from the initial stage known as Kutichaka. In this stage, they eat food at least twice a day. As the stages get elevated, with the degree of dispassion becoming more and more intense, stages like Param Hansa are reached by the saint. In the stage of Param Hansa, they eat very little food and do not find any difference between soil and gold (Mitti and Sona). When all these stages are surpassed, then the saint is termed as Avadhuta. Bhagwan Dattatray is an Avadhuta.

==

When the saint reaches the stage of Avadhuta, owing to the enquiry of their own Swaroop, they become the knower of the various secrets of this illusive world. Then only they leave holding the staff and kamandal. They also leave wearing the katisutra (a thread surrounding the waist) and all other clothes. They do not wear any clothes. This is the reason they are also called Digambara. They do not even use the bark of the trees to cover their body. They neither shave nor take a bath. They live beyond all good, bad, punya, papa (sin), worship of God etc. They do not get involved in the worldly and Vedic rituals. They are beyond all dualities: happiness-sorrow, hot-cold, respect-disrespect etc. They remain in a state of extreme desirelessness. They are free from all vices like attachment, greed, anger, and the like. They are egoless. They think that their body is dead for all purposes. This is why they have no fear of death. They do not care for the protection of their body because their minds are rested in the Soul. Like animals, whatever they get as food, they eat. They remain fully refrained from all sorts of greediness. They think education and knowledge are illusive, so they leave these thinking to be dust. They imagine the best and the non-dual image of the Lord. They think, "There is nothing beyond me. I am the Purna Brahma." They think that the Self is the epilogue of all Gods and the Gurus. Accordingly, they never feel unhappy in adverse circumstances nor do they feel happy in favourable situations. They remain away from attachment and never have affection or love towards the auspicious-inauspicious. All their Indriyas maintain austerities. They never think of their past births nor welcome the dharmas of Varnashramas. For them, days and nights are alike. They hardly take rest. They spend their time moving around mostly. They never become carefree. They have left everything except their body. They always remain isolated. They treat the land and water as their kamandal. They are never excited. They are very calm in their nature. They remain silent and keep their minds in the pure Brahman always. They forget everything and remain very dependent on themselves (Atmanishtha).

This state of the Avadhuta is known as Turiyattita. They are absorbed in the thought of the Super Soul, having deep meditation on Pranab (OM). With this Turiyattita state, they leave their body in this world.

OM Tat Sat!

The spiritual aspirants should try their best to realise God and be free.

God bless all.

May all sentient beings be at peace, may no one suffer from illness;

May all see what is auspicious, may no one suffer.

Om Shantih! Shantih!! Shantih!!!